IN THE SHADOW OF LOVE

In the Shadow *of* Love

Stories from My Life

ℐ

WALTER MEYERHOF

PROFESSOR OF PHYSICS EMERITUS
STANFORD UNIVERSITY

2002 · FITHIAN PRESS, SANTA BARBARA, CALIFORNIA

Published by Fithian Press
A division of Daniel and Daniel, Publishers, Inc.
Post Office Box 1525
Santa Barbara, CA 93102

LIBRARY OF CONGRESS CATALOGING-IN-PUBLICATION DATA
Meyerhof, Walter E. (Walter Ernst) [date]
  In the shadow of love : stories from my life / by Walter Meyerhof.
    p. cm.
  ISBN 1-56474-393-4 (alk. paper)
  1. Meyerhof, Walter E. (Walter Ernst), [date] 2. Jews—Germany—Berlin—
Biography. 3. Physicists—United States—Biography. 4. Refugees, Jewish—
Biography. I. Title.
  DS135.G5 M49 2002
  943'.155087'092—dc21

                    2001004471

To Miriam

and to those who
wish to know more about me

CONTENTS

Preface

IN THE FALL OF 2000 and the following winter quarter, I took a Foothill College (Palo Alto, CA) extension course called Life Stories, for persons over sixty who wanted to write about their life for their descendents. The teacher was Sheila Dunec, who for the past three years taught this course. Each quarter, the outline of the course is more or less the same, starting with the subject of artifacts one has inherited, continuing to the progression of one's life from birth to the present, and ending with more general topics such as accomplishments, coping with death in the family, simplifying one's life as one gets older. Since one was not bound by the suggested subjects, I chose to write only about my life and to touch peripherally on more general topics as they occurred in my life.

In this collection, I have ordered the stories more or less chronologically, but since each story was written to be read aloud in class, not always to the same audience, some events in the past or the future are told in more than one story to make each story stand by itself. Typically, after a first draft, I revised each story 10 to 15 times before I was "satisfied." This seems to be a never ending process, because each time I reread a story, I change a few words more and the date of this collection.

My gratitude goes to Sheila for nourishing my writing with encouragement, as a result of which I had a lot of fun and satisfaction writing these stories. I thank Miriam for her constructive suggestions and for tolerating my endless thinking and talking about these stories as they were written. I am very grateful to Norma Lundholm Djerassi for her thoughtful comments, to my sister-in-law Susi Meyerhof for numerous corrections, and to my sister Bettina Emerson for recollecting many stories from my youth better than I.

Menlo Park, July 2001

IN THE SHADOW OF LOVE

ILLUSTRERAD · TIDNING

IDUN

FÖR · KVINNAN · OCH · HEMMET

GRUNDLAGD AV
FRITHIOF HELLBERG

UTGIVARE:
BEYRON CARLSSON

UPPLAGA **A**

N:o **47**

DEN 25 NOV. 1923

PRIS 35 ÖRE

REDAKTÖR
EBBA THEORIN

En Nobelpristagares hustru.

Fru Hedwig Meyerhof, gift med No-
belpristagaren i medicin prof.
Meyerhof i Kiel, är så som
en ung flicka och ej
heller så värst myc-
ket äldre.

1. Cover Portrait

BEFORE ME LIE A SWEDISH woman's magazine from 1923 and a new Swedish–English dictionary. The magazine is called *IDUN, Illustrated Magazine for Women and the Home*. The cover of the magazine shows the posed photograph of a seated woman in her thirties. Her dark hair is parted in the middle. Her gaze seems to be directed both outward and inward. Her lips are closed. She wears an elegant dark dress with long sleeves and a shimmering belt, but what I find most striking are her hands. Her left hand, with a ring on the middle finger, holds back gently the first three fingers of her right hand, leaving the other fingers loose on her thigh, as if to say she is finding it difficult to hold on to all the facets of her life.

I want to understand this woman better and try to read the short article in the magazine about the cover picture. Swedish must be one of the most complex European languages, because I manage to decipher only a few of the phrases. Fortunately, I found the name of a local lady who married a Swedish man, and she graciously agreed to translate the article. Since it is short, I give it in its entirety at the end of this story. Here, I quote only a couple of sentences: "...a thirty-year old lady, combines in her person a soulful beauty with intelligence and gentle motherhood, and it is a charming picture to see this lovely German mother, surrounded by lovely children. In the beginning somewhat shy because of all the attention which has suddenly come her way, she gave us some information about their current life...."

A photo in the article shows the same woman on a chair, wearing a short-sleeved dress. On her lap sits an 18-month-old baby boy in a night shirt. A seven-year-old boy is standing on one side of her, and a five-year-old girl on the other. All the children are smiling brightly, as if the photographer had just said "cheese," and the woman has a gentle smile. Her lips are slightly drawn in.

The woman is my mother, and the baby boy is me. The others are my brother Gottfried and my sister Bettina.

The article also has a photo of my father's face, with a positive look and slight dimples which I have inherited. He is nearly forty years old. The article says nothing about his birth into the family of a prominent Jewish textile dealer in Hanover, nothing about his fragile health as a young man which required a year-long trip to the dry climate of Egypt, nothing about his study of medicine, and his deep interest since his student days in psychiatry, philosophy, poetry, literature, and art.

Believing that many psychiatric problems are related to bodily problems, he became interested in physiology. Encouraged by an older colleague, he was soon led to a subject he found more fascinating than psychiatry, the study of the complex chemical reactions which make the movement of muscles possible, and for which eventually he received the Nobel prize in 1922. The award of the 1922 Nobel prizes was delayed until 1923 by the aftermath of the Russian revolution following World War I.

The article in *IDUN* briefly describes my mother's life. Born in

1891, in Cologne, as the youngest of five children in a Jewish grocer's family, she was the only one of her siblings who turned to a life of the intellect. At the age of 17 she started taking courses in physics and mathematics at the University of Heidelberg at a time when this was most unusual for a woman. She must have found the inner strength and determination to follow her interests then and later in her life. Education was esteemed in Jewish families and as the youngest child she managed to follow her imagination and her own wishes.

In the mathematics course at the university, she met my father, seven years her senior, who was then pursuing postgraduate studies. Both of them continued their studies at various universities in Germany, finally meeting in Kiel where in 1913 my father had obtained a position as a Research Assistant to a Professor of Physiology. In between, they had many encounters. A photograph from 1911 shows my mother as the only woman among 15 men in the circle of a German philosopher, Leonard Nelson. Nelson believed strongly in bringing the benefits of education to the working class. My father was greatly influenced by him. He taught classes for working people during his studies in Heidelberg and he extended Nelson's social philosophy by also volunteering as a doctor for poor people. Later, for a while, he cared for German soldiers wounded in the First World War.

My parents married six years after they had first met, in June 1914, shortly before the outbreak of World War I.

The article in the women's magazine does not refer to any grandparents because they had passed away before I was born, and it fails to mention a sixth member of our family, Anni. After the birth of my brother in 1916 and my sister in 1918, my mother felt she needed help with the children. Anni had served as governess to a German military attaché in China, who was returning to Germany at the end of the war and no longer needed her, and she was ready for a new job. My mother took her on, not foreseeing that she would stay in our family for 14 years.

After I was born in 1922, my mother had a severe postpartum depression. Checking herself into a sanatorium, she began seeking professional help which, on and off, continued throughout her life. I think she found it difficult to cope not only with her children, but also with her life in general. As a grocer's daughter, she had married up in status. Her husband was seven years older and he was immensely talented in many areas. How could she keep up? Two decades later, she sometimes came to me at night, tearfully, saying she had been a bad wife and companion to my father. I put my arm around her to console her and to point out the contrary reality.

So, since my birth Anni cradled me, bathed me, changed my diapers, played with me, walked me, and then encouraged me to stand upright. I have several photos with her cuddling me and looking at me, ignoring my brother and sister standing nearby. Unable to ever bear children, she treated me like her own child. As I became older, she told me I would lose my mother's affection if I behaved badly, thereby pulling me even closer to her for protection.

Yet, here was my real mother also, and my feelings towards both the women in my life became muddled. Although my mother read me bedtime stories, why was she not taking care of me all the time? When I asked Anni, she implied that would be too much of a burden for my mother. I felt guilty, later wondering whether I had been "a mistake." Even now I try to please the women I encounter in my life, hoping to avoid rejection.

§

Once more, I glance at the portrait on the magazine cover. Would the journalist who wrote the article about the picture have known the Swedish expressions for the feelings of a baby boy seeking the embracing warmth of his mother and her loving gaze upon him, but finding that both were escaping him? I open the dictionary and search for the words.

IDUN ARTICLE, November 25, 1923

The beautiful portrait which decorates this number's cover, *IDUN'S* correspondent obtained during a private visit at the home in Kiel of Nobel Prize winner in medicine, Professor Otto Meyerhof. Frau Hedwig Meyerhof, a thirty-year-old lady, combines in her person a soulful beauty with intelligence and gentle motherhood, and it is a charming picture to see this lovely German mother, surrounded by lovely children. In the beginning somewhat shy, she gave us some information about their current life. Frau Meyerhof who was born in Cologne, after finishing high school, went to Heidelberg University to study mathematics and physics. It was there that she met her present husband. In 1914, the war year, they were married, and the young wife studied several semesters in Munich, Berlin, and Göttingen. The marriage began during the very serious circumstances at that time in Germany, and already as a new bride Frau Meyerhof served as a nurse in the Red Cross.

"Then I had my three children," finished Frau Meyerhof, with a tender glance towards the children's room. "My housewifely duties take all my time. Therefore, I can't actively help my husband in his work. That my husband got the Nobel Prize has naturally been a great happiness both for us personally and in our capacity as German citizens."

Translated by Olive Borgsteadt

2. Chicken House

MY FATHER'S PHOTO ALBUM is open to the page which holds a picture of the chicken house in our backyard in Berlin. The photo dates from about 1926 when I was four years old. Our family had moved to Berlin from Kiel two years earlier, and the chicken house was at the back of the property. A fence separated it from a wooded area back of the lot.

Eggs were a delicacy in Germany. My mother wanted my father to have a fresh egg every morning. So after the chicken house was built, a dozen chickens were bought, two roosters and the rest hens. Each morning, the eggs were taken, but one night thieves climbed over the back fence and stole all the chickens, except for two hens. The police found their heads and feathers in the woods. Since the remaining hens could not lay enough eggs, they were slaughtered for a Sunday meal. After that, we three children used the chicken house as a play house.

The photo shows my brother and me sitting on the roof, together with the daughter of the photographer holding our cat Mulli. (All our cats were named Mulli.) My sister is standing on a ladder leaning against the roof, holding flowers. Sometimes, she held a garden hose with water squirting out. We had to jump off the roof over or under the arc of water without getting wet. It was great fun, until one day water spilled on the roof and I slipped and fell to the ground, luckily without any permanent damage. That ended the jumping.

The chicken house also served us as a lookout into the woods behind the fence. We told each other that we had spied white hooded ghosts back there, romping around among the trees. We speculated what the ghosts might be doing during the day and at night, not realizing that the woods belonged to a hospital for disabled children who had to wear white uniforms.

For me, the time spent with my siblings was special. They were so much older than I was—four and six years—and to be included in their activities was a treat. I remember an equal feeling of closeness when my brother agreed, after some begging, to pull me in the street in a *Leiterwagen*, a wooden four-wheeled cart with ladder-like sides. The cart had separately hinged front wheels, connected to a steering rod. On an incline, one could sit in the cart and steer the cart, but near us all the streets were flat and I was out of luck.

On one occasion, my brother egged me on to climb over the garden gate facing the street to show that I was now a "big" boy who did not need to be pulled anymore. The gate was topped with barbed wire against burglars. As I tried to climb over, I tore a gash on the inside left elbow. It had to be stitched. I still have a scar.

As the fall season approached, the weather became quite miserable in Berlin. Memories of those times have faded, but photographs show us children dressing up from time to time to put on little plays for our parents and our nanny Anni.

In Berlin, my mother engaged Anni's younger sister Hermine as a cook and maid. With growing children and their increasing activities, more help was needed in the household. For me, Anni was still the loving mother figure she had been earlier in Kiel, but she also became a stricter disciplinarian: not only would I lose my mother's love if I misbehaved, but she would call the policeman, if I lied to her. My sister remembers similar warnings.

As Christmas approached, we prepared our Christmas play. We were going to be dressed up as the three wise men, speaking a few lines our father had prepared. When it came to the actual performance, I had forgotten some of my lines and felt terribly embarrassed.

Although both my parents came from Jewish families, soon after their marriage in 1914 they thought, as many German intellectuals did, that their children would adapt better to German life and culture if they were baptized. They left their Jewish congregation and chose the prevalent, Lutheran religion for their children. So for us, Christmas was the natural winter holiday.

In the first years, Anni and my mother prepared the Christmas tree. Real candles were used, with some tinsel and ornaments. Sometimes, a nativity scene was built under the tree.

I became aware of a regular Christmas routine. I was told that Father Christmas had come through the chimney and had brought presents, and indeed soon the door opened and Father Christmas appeared. On his head was a red cap with a fuzzy pendant and he wore a big mustache and large glasses. He was draped in a white sheet. In his hands were some papers from which he read a long poem, describing what each member of the family had done during the past year, praising and admonishing. One poem asked me not to climb over the garden gate anymore.

I was wondering how it was possible for Father Christmas to come down the chimney without getting dirty and was told that he could make himself very thin as he went through.

After Father Christmas left, we were allowed to unwrap the presents he had brought and which had been covered with a sheet while the poem was read. Finally, a meal was served in which a large carp was the main dish. It was the ultimate delicacy. The dessert often was a *Mehlkloss*, a steamed dough made with flour and eggs, studded with raisins, and bathed in a vanilla sauce. If I happen to be in Germany now, I still try to find this dessert and think back to my childhood days.

After a few years I noticed that my father always disappeared before the Christmas ceremony and I asked Anni. She said he had to go to the bathroom and would soon be back. My, I thought, he is taking a long time! Finally, at age ten, I was told the truth, to the hilarious laughter of my brother and sister, making fun of my gullibility and greatly discomforting me.

In 1928, a year before we moved to Heidelberg, at age six, I was brought to my first elementary school. I went with a *Zuckertüte*, a conical cardboard bag filled with sweets which one could start eating during the first hour if the teacher allowed, as my teacher did. Miss Müller, who had a private school, was a very gentle lady. I was happy in her class.

I remember discussions between my mother and Anni, who would take me to school the first time. They agreed that my mother would bring me first, but that Anni could take and fetch me thereafter. These discussions were the first clouds that slowly gathered. Four years later, my mother finally asserted herself and dismissed Anni, saying the children no longer needed a nanny.

By the time we moved to Heidelberg, the chicken house had lost its appeal, but I wistfully took a last look at it when I left. I wondered whether other children would move into our house. Would they climb up on the chicken house and spy ghosts in the woods behind?

3. My Father's Gold Pocket Watch

AS FAR AS I REMEMBER from my childhood days, my father always wore a vest, whether it was hot or cold. Otherwise, he would not have known what time it was, because he never wore a wristwatch. He owned a gold pocket watch, attached to a chain, the other end of which could be clasped to a button on his vest or through a button hole. The watch was in the left vest pocket.

My sister, who is four years older than I, remembers that in the early 1930s, when we were living in Heidelberg, my father once went to the bathroom. For some reason, he bent over and the pocket watch, which he had inherited from his father, slipped into the toilet. In those times, toilet drains went straight down. Absent-mindedly, my father also flushed, so the watch was lost forever, because one did not know where in the drain pipe it might be lying. After a long period of sorrow and discussion, my father decided to buy a new gold watch, one with Arabic numerals instead of the Roman ones on the old watch.

I am holding this watch in my hand. Its thin chain is particularly long. When I wound it up the other day, it started ticking—

after more than fifty years. Maybe, it wanted to tell me a story.

Out of the blue, in 1987, a Miss Reynal wrote to me from Perpignan, a town in southern France, where she was living as a retired school teacher. In her letter, written in French, she enclosed the clipping of an article from a local paper, which she had just read.

The article described an interview by a journalist with Lisa Fittko, herself a German refugee who, with her now deceased husband, had tried to help me and others escape from France in 1940. Lisa Fittko mentioned that I was now a physicist at Stanford University and that my father was Otto Meyerhof, Nobel Prize winner in 1922.

In 1940, my father had brought my mother and me to Banyuls-sur-Mer, a small village at the foot of the Pyrenees mountains. Since the Vichy government had refused him an exit visa, without which one could not leave France legally, he had hoped to escape from there to Spain and then to the U.S. As a cover for being in Banyuls, my father had himself assigned to work at the local Marine Biological Laboratory as a biochemical researcher.

Miss Reynal wrote that she had grown up in Banyuls-sur-Mer. Her letter read in part:

> The article in the paper brought back memories from 1940. I still see before me the patio of the restaurant Oms at Banyuls. Each day a gentleman, researcher at the Laboratory, came for lunch, seated next to a table occupied by a couple of boys and girls who attended the village school. They were carefree, despite the tragic times, and laughed a lot about nothing. They found their neighbor sympathetic and tried to engage him in small talk. As often as they could, they would ask him for the time, only to be able to observe how he would take hold of a chain at-

tached to his watch and pull the watch out of his vest pocket.

Miss Reynal evidently was confused between me and my father, because her letter continues:

> We found your presence in Banyuls unusual. We knew you were not French and thought you were hiding in the French Free Zone, far from the Gestapo. When, in November 1942, the first German tanks arrived behind the swastika flags, I hid at home and cried, thinking that France had been completely crushed by the Nazi juggernaut. We had waited in vain for several days in the restaurant for our sympathetic table neighbor. We thought often about you and wondered whether you had escaped from the Nazi horde.
>
> Thanks to the article in the paper, I think I now know the answer. I believe that Mr. Meyerhof, Professor at Stanford University, had been our sympathetic neighbor at the next table. I am happy you survived that terrible period. I won't conceal from you that when I went for walks in Banyuls I often wondered, what has happened to him?

Miss Reynal's letter got me interested again in my father's gold watch and in Banyuls. When I visited there recently, I tried to locate the restaurant where my father went for lunch sixty years ago. The restaurant is gone, but the square on which its patio was located is still there, as is the laboratory where he had worked.

Actually, my father and mother had been guided across the Pyrenees already in October 1940, long before the Germans occupied the French Free Zone. They arrived in Philadelphia at the end of the same month. A research position at the University of

Pennsylvania was waiting for my father. I arrived half a year later, after my parents had arranged for my immigration visa.

My father died in 1951, and my mother in '54. My father would have been as amused by Miss Reynal's letter as I was, perhaps pulling the gold watch out of his vest pocket once more to check the time.

4. The Microscope

I OPEN THE LEATHER CASE and pull out the microscope. Its stand is neatly folded and its tube is pushed together. I unfold the stand and pull out the tube. Now the microscope looks exactly as it did when I took a picture of it 66 years ago. My parents had given it to me for my twelfth birthday.

I was curious about everything: what did my fingernails look like when I magnified them, or the grain of wood, or a feather, or squashed flies and mosquitoes?

It was 1934. We had been in Heidelberg for five years. Even though the *Volksschule*, the elementary school, had been shockingly different from what I had experienced in my last year in Berlin, one of the teachers had stimulated my curiosity. But, during breaks, we all had to walk in circles, the boys in one direction and the girls in the opposite direction. One was allowed to go out of the circle only with permission, to go to the bathroom. I did that as often as I could.

I was so happy when, after two years, I could change schools to go to *Gymnasium* which my sister and my brother attended. This secondary school provided a nine-year education in classics and the sciences, which eventually could lead to university admission.

In the second or the third year, the geography professor gave me his entire collection of minerals, stored in a dark brown cabinet with many drawers. He could no longer use it in his teaching. One day, he had opened one of the drawers to let me take a look at the neat rows of boxed rocks, some with crystalline outcrops and each neatly labeled. I was intrigued by the regular shapes of crystals. When I asked the teacher later several times to show me other drawers, he saw that I was fascinated. I still have feelings of affection for polished rocks and for crystals and have several on my desk and shelves.

Hitler came to power in Germany in 1933 and the increasingly pernicious influence of his political philosophy was soon felt in the schools. When a teacher entered the classroom, we had to stand up and give the Nazi salute saying *"Heil Hitler."* I just moved my lips and did not say anything.

Among my few good friends was Werner, the son of a Jewish pharmacist. Once, we quarreled and, to annoy him, I painted a swastika on his desk. When I told my parents, they were shocked. They asked me whether I did not know that my background was Jewish, and they pointed out what a repulsive thing I had done. Since they had brought me up as a Lutheran, I had assumed our family background was Christian. Even though my parents never went to church, my nanny Anni took me along each Sunday. They had never talked about our background. Nevertheless, I was very ashamed at what I had done and felt terribly guilty, a guilt feeling that stayed with me for over sixty years. When I saw Werner half a century later—he had since moved to Brazil—I asked him after some hesitancy whether he remembered the swastika I had painted on his desk. He did not know what I was talking about.

By the end of 1933, a Hitler Youth group had formed at the

school. One very tall boy, whom I can still recognize in a class photo, was their leader. He asked me why I was at "their" school and
that "they" would beat me up in gym class if I persisted in coming.
I felt terrorized and turned to my older brother, who was in his last
year in the Gymnasium, for protection. He said he could not help
me.

In music class, I once kept on singing my part of a canon at
the wrong time. The teacher got so mad that he came up to me
and slapped my face so hard that my nose bled. When my parents
complained to the principal the next day, he indicated he was powerless because the music teacher was a member of the Nazi party.

Except for school, my life in Heidelberg at first was not greatly affected by the Nazi atmosphere. At home, I had a sunny room
leading to a large balcony. I have a picture of me sitting at a table
with my stuffed animals lined up and another one with a large
wood plane in my arms. I don't remember what I did with it, but I
have always loved working with wood. Later, in school in England,
I turned wooden bowls on a lathe, shaping and hollowing out
blocks glued together with differently colored wooden pieces.

One Christmas, my parents gave me a chemistry set with
which I experimented in a basement room. My brother often
joined me. One afternoon, we decided to electrolyze water using a
bundle of flashlight batteries and a large bell jar to collect the gas-
es. Suddenly, an explosion shattered the jar. Luckily, all the pieces
missed us.

In the basement also, our parents had stored some paintings
by a well-known artist, Gertrud Jacob. She was a psychiatrist by
profession, and sometimes painted her young patients. She had
also painted me, holding an apple, when I was about three years
old. My brother and sister said that I looked deranged and egged
me on to kick in the painting, which I did with mixed feelings of
superiority and concern. We hid the painting among the others.

When the tear in the painting was later discovered, my father called us into his study, one by one, and scolded each of us severely, which was rare for him. He had the picture repaired at a considerable cost.

One morning, I could not find my cat Mulli. I searched frantically through the three floors of our house. Finally, I looked in the coal cellar. There lay Mulli on some pieces of coal. I called out to her, but she did not respond. For the first time in my life I faced the stillness of death. After a full burial in the garden and a long period of mourning, another Mulli was provided by my uncle Franz who was a cat lover and supplied us with Mullis when needed. Often, when Mulli was not around, I played with our dog, Schlucki. He was a gentle, ugly, bulldoggish creature with a miniature tail which wagged when strangers came to the house. I think his mother never taught him how to bark.

On weekends we went for walks in the hills around Heidelberg. A photo of the outing was often taken, which, as I became older, I hated so much that I turned around. But for *Fasching*, a Halloween-like holiday, we all dressed up. I was a clown, and did not mind having my picture taken.

Winters were spent in the Swiss Alps in a region called the Engadin, where the terrain is not too steep. I loved tobogganing with my brother and sister, and learned skating and skiing. Not being a daredevil, I never skied well, but I continued both sports whenever I could and enjoyed them greatly until I was seventy, when the fear of falling took the upper hand.

Once a year we had a dreaded visitor, my father's widowed friend Lotte with whom he shared an intense interest in poetry and literature. As far as we children were concerned, her specialty was table manners: how to hold the knife properly, the fork, and the spoon, how to eat without making a noise, how to sit, where to put the hands. Her criticisms were sharp and could be hurtful. When she was around, Schlucki was banned from the dining room, because all he could do was to sit and drool during mealtime. We were so happy when Lotte left. Now we could continue our little mealtime games, such as hiding a piece of wiener sausage (which we considered a delicacy) in our napkins and pulling it out and eating it at the last moment saying "He who laughs last, laughs best." We did not foresee that several years later, Lotte would be transported to Auschwitz and be murdered there.

My adolescent years in Heidelberg came to an end in 1936. In that year, after a three-year process, my father's honorary position at the University of Heidelberg was terminated because of his Jewish background. He realized Hitler's rule would not be short lived, as he had always thought. The following year, he visited the U.S. to find a position, but nothing which he considered suitable turned up. He could not tear himself away from the superb research facilities available to him at the Kaiser-Wilhelm Institute in Heidelberg, which had allowed him the most productive period of his scientific life. A dozen research assistants had worked with him, nearly half of whom later received the Nobel prize.

For the summer holiday of 1936, my parents decided to send me to England to a family which took in Jewish children, instead of packing me off to a camp in Germany, as in previous years. I quickly took English lessons, so I could make the trip by myself.

A new life began for me at age 14. It is amazing that I and the microscope have survived. I really had wanted to give it to my grandson for his twelfth birthday, but for some reason it is still here. So, I fold it up gently and put it back on my shelf in its leather case. It will wait there patiently until I unpack it once more and think back to my years in Heidelberg.

5. The Old School Tie

THE OLD SCHOOL TIE always hung far inside my closet on the last peg of the tie rack. It had dark and light blue stripes, separated by thin white ones. When I looked for it the other day, I couldn't find it. I guess I really didn't want to be reminded of my life in England from 1936 to 1938, a time which did not bring me much happiness, although it taught me that fate, with a little bit of nudging, can sometimes convert adversity into advantage. I also learned that through will power one can often achieve one's goals, a lesson which has helped me in my professional life.

I came to Dulwich College, London, by accident. My parents had sent me to the family of Dr. Singer for a few weeks' summer holiday in 1936 when I was 14. Dr. Charles Singer, a science historian, was known and recommended by my father's English Nobel Prize co-recipient and friend A.V. Hill. The Singers had a country house in Cornwall, England, and accepted a few Jewish children from Germany to give them a brief respite from the Nazi atmosphere. Also, they were company for the Singers' two teenage children, a girl and a boy. We went swimming, sightseeing, hiking, and talked about our lives. Toward the end of my stay, Mrs. Singer asked me:

"Do you really want to go back to Germany, where the Nazi boys at school will bully you probably even more than before? Why don't you go to school in England?"

It took me a few days to think about this. I phoned my parents. They were in favor, and noted that my older brother was living in London. He had left Heidelberg two years earlier to study Civil Engineering at University College. And, we had distant relatives in London, because one of my father's aunts had married into an English family. Also, a cousin of my father lived in London.

So, I decided to accept Mrs. Singer's suggestion. She immediately phoned around to find a school which would still accept me so late in the summer. She located two schools, one in London and one outside. I picked the one in London and went home to pack some clothes and other items required by the school for boarders. The school was Dulwich College, a boys' high school with a good reputation. I was amazed that I had been accepted, because all my grades from the *Gymnasium* in Heidelberg were only "good" or "sufficient." I had never worked very hard and, according to a comment by the principal on my final grade report, "was not always fully concentrated."

Dulwich College accepted day students from nearby areas and some boarders, around one thousand in all. The half-a-dozen Boarding Houses were each run by a Headmaster, typically married. A Matron looked after the health and nourishment of the boarders. The Headmaster of our house, Mr. Taylor, was a former army man, a bit regimental. Discipline among the twenty-odd students in the house was kept by three Prefects who were older students. The other students were divided into Seniors and Juniors. The Prefects slept in single rooms, the Juniors and Seniors in a dormitory.

I was admitted to the house as a Junior. I had to open the door for any Prefect, address him as "Sir," and do whatever he asked me to do. Also, as a Junior, I had to wear a plain black tie and had to let any Senior pass through a door first.

Dorm talk at night was a new experience for me. We had been told by the Matron that anyone caught talking after "lights out" would be severely punished, but after half an hour of silent waiting for a check-up by a Prefect, some Seniors began softly spoken stories about the female anatomy and their interactions with it. The stories became more descriptive as the nights went by. I was confused and intrigued since neither my nanny Anni nor my parents had ever broached the subject. I had no one I could talk with. When I went home that Christmas, I sneaked into my father's study and looked at some anatomy books on his shelves. The medical language related only vaguely to the dorm talk, but there was no other way to deal with my confusion and curiosity.

One evening, at the end of November, two months after I had arrived at Dulwich, everybody ran out of the house to watch a hill near the horizon which was lit by a huge fire. Soon the word spread, "Crystal Palace is on fire." One housemate explained that Crystal Palace had been built, mainly of glass, for the Great World Exhibition of 1851 and had still been in use, and what a loss its destruction was for the English. Not particularly liking the British school system, I did not express any sympathy.

I made up my mind to get better grades in the English school than in Germany and spent a lot of time on homework, even when the other boys went out to play or stayed indoors and relaxed with games or talked. The Headmaster called me into his office and scolded me, but I told him it was a sacrifice for my father to pay tuition and board for me in England (approximately $500 per year) despite currency restrictions. I just had to do well. Thereafter, I was left alone, but some Seniors made remarks about me, including anti-Semitic ones.

On weekends, I escaped as often as I could. I was allowed to leave only if I had an invitation from some person, who then had to sign a permission slip, confirming that the visit had indeed taken place. The slip was handed out on Friday and had to be returned no later than Monday. The London postal service was so good that I could mail the slip to my brother on Friday and it came back to me on Monday. On Sunday, I would visit the huge Science Museum in London and amuse myself by turning knobs and watching demonstrations, often eating fish and chips for lunch.

If I was not able to leave, I had to go to chapel with the other boys and sing and pray and listen to interminable sermons. In winter, we amused ourselves by playing football on the muddy grass; in the summer it was cricket. I was not very good at either, but tried to give a passable performance.

After a couple of months, I was fed up wearing a plain black tie on my outings into town. I went to the Dulwich store and bought the nicely colored school tie. On the suburban train, I changed ties in the toilet to avoid being seen. I must have told one of the more friendly boys in house, and in turn he told one of the nastier ones who mentioned it to one of the Prefects. After a "hearing" by all the Prefects, I was told that I had violated tradition. The tie would be confiscated and I would receive ten strokes with a wooden paddle on my naked bottom. I thought that I had exchanged the Nazi bullies in Germany for the Prefect bullies in England. This was more hurtful than the actual paddling even though my skin was bleeding afterwards and had to be dressed by the Matron.

Toward the end of the first school year, I applied for Senior status and, after a lengthy interview by the Prefects, was accepted. I bought another tie.

For the summer months, I went home to Heidelberg. Upon entering Germany, I had to wear a yellow cloth star, indicating my

Jewish background. I wore it as sloppily as I could, but was not bothered by the German border police.

My parents had given me a tent as a birthday present, and now I put it up, together with one of my former school friends. First we slept in it in our garden, and then our parents allowed us to go for a two-night overnight trip on the river Neckar which flows through Heidelberg. Our family had a *Faltboot*, a two-seater kayak with rubberized skin held taut by wooden rods and a bottom plank. In the evening, the boat could be disassembled, the rods packed together, the plank folded, the skin rolled up and all put into a rucksack, with the paddle pieces sticking out, but we did not bother. We just pulled the boat up on the shore for the night, put up the tent and enjoyed frying wieners over an open flame.

When the second year at Dulwich College started in September 1937, I felt better adapted. I concentrated on preparing for the final school examination the following year. Once in a while, I visited one of our relatives. One family had a beach house in Brighton. I remember a romantic walk in the evening along the beach with a distant cousin, for the first time in my life holding hands with a girl. It was a very pleasant feeling.

The physics teacher at Dulwich was particularly friendly to me and allowed me to do experiments with school equipment outside of regular class hours. I spent entire afternoons in his laboratory. His encouragement led me to choose physics as a profession, rather than chemistry which I had also considered.

In July 1938, I took the "Oxford and Cambridge School Certificate" examination. I passed with "credit" in all subjects, indicating high grades. This would have permitted me to attend any university in England, except for the fact that I was too young, barely 16. I would have had to wait for two years.

In the summer, I went home to Heidelberg. My father finally decided to leave Germany at the end of the summer. A research position had been found for him in Paris by friends there. My mother urged me to go to Berlin for a month, to discuss my inner turmoil about sex with a professional who had a very good reputation. She felt unable to help me. Since my sister was studying in Berlin at the time, I agreed.

In Berlin, I was occupied only one hour a day talking with a psychiatrist and I looked for ways to keep me busy. I called the daughter of one of my mother's closest friends, who from time to time had accompanied her mother to Heidelberg as a child. She had played mainly with my sister, but now she was a beautiful young lady. Her name was Miriam Ruben. After a couple of visits, I asked her out for a date. She said to me *"Du bist ein dummer Affe"* ("You are a dumb ape"), so I went out with her roommate instead. We did not foresee that nine years later we would meet again, in London, fall in love, and go through the rest of our lives together.

When I returned to Heidelberg, I helped to get everything packed we could take on our pretend vacation in Switzerland, which would precede the emigration to France. Much had to be left behind, including my beloved collection of rocks and crystals which had given me so much pleasure. I gave it to a friend. Because it would take some time for my parents to get settled in Paris, it was decided that I should return to Dulwich College for the winter quarter and join my parents in Paris at Christmas 1938. There, I would prepare for the entrance examination for an advanced school in Paris, where I could study physics, and my young age did not matter.

In Dulwich, I found out that my former boarding house was going to be sold. It had been privately owned by the Headmaster, as several boarding houses at Dulwich were. He had run it for profit. No wonder the miserable meals we had been fed, except for weekends when some parents might suddenly be visiting! I was transferred to another house whose Headmaster was a reverend of the Church of England. He had given some of the boring sermons in chapel I was forced to attend on Sundays, but he was friendly, even if somewhat humorless. In view of my good academic work, he offered me the position of Head Prefect, but since I hated the Prefect system, I declined, even though I missed out on a private room.

I felt that I had worked extremely hard for two years, and now was the time for some relaxation. I studied only enough not to fail the courses, and some of my teachers were quite disgusted by my changed attitude. I did not mind, but in order not to dishonor the Old School Tie, I did not wear it anymore. The tie didn't care; nevertheless, I held on to it for many years as a reluctant memory of my meandering travels toward adulthood.

6. Edith

"TWO STEPS FORWARD, one step to the right," the dancing instructor impatiently repeated as she was trying to teach us the fox-trot. My dancing partner was a slender girl. She tried her best to follow my hesitant steps. I asked for her name. "Edith," she said, looking shyly at the floor. The next week, she came again and I gently inquired whether she would like to dance with me again. She agreed. Slowly we told each other what we were doing.

She was 14, going to school. I had just come from England before Christmas and was living with my parents in Paris. I attended a preparatory school for the entrance examination to the Ecole de Physique et de Chimie Industrielles de la Ville de Paris (School of Industrial Physics and Chemistry of the City of Paris), where I hoped to study physics. It was January 1939. I was 16.

After a few weeks, I hinted to Edith that I would enjoy having a coffee with her sometime. She said she would first have to ask her parents. The following week she reported that her parents wanted to meet me. Edith said her mother was easygoing, but that her father was very strict, so when a few days later I climbed up the dark stairs to their apartment on the Boulevard Montparnasse, I was tense. I had put on a dark suit and a dark tie.

Edith's mother invited me for coffee and cookies and tried to put me at ease. Her father, of smallish stature, had a pince-nez. He was a functionary in the city administration. He stayed only a few minutes. Soon I left, doubting that I had made a good impression on her father. At the following dancing lesson, Edith confirmed my suspicions. Even though her mother was favorable, her father did not want her to go out with me. I asked Edith whether her father might be willing to have a longer interview with me. It took about two weeks for Edith to arrange a second interview with the help of her mother. I learned that persistence sometimes pays off.

I climbed the stairs again, this time thinking I would not be so easily defeated again. Edith's father questioned me as if I might be a potential son-in-law. I outlined my plans to work for an advanced degree in physics, with the aim of teaching and research or possibly joining an industrial enterprise. It became clear that this man disliked my German and my Jewish backgrounds, even though he mentioned that he had Jewish friends. These feelings were balanced by the fact that I was *"le fils d'un prix Nobel"* (the son of a Nobel prize winner), a phrase I carefully dropped, although generally had avoided using.

At the following dancing lesson, Edith told me that her father had relented and that we could go out together under the condition that her younger brother come along as our chaperon. Also, she had to be back home one hour before dinner. The first quickie kiss did not occur until many weeks later when the brother wasn't looking. By then, he had become very bored with his duty and consented to make himself available only because I surreptitiously paid him a few francs for each hour he spent with us.

My preparatory school, Ecole Lavoisier, was located conveniently close to our apartment. The homework was very difficult, often taking until two or three o'clock in the morning. I had missed the first semester of the school year and my knowledge of French was based on just two years of courses taken at Dulwich College in London. I was familiar with most of the subject matter, but was challenged by the French habit of labeling all processes in physics and chemistry, and the main equations in mathematics, with the names of French scientists who supposedly discovered them.

Despite my father's love of philosophy, I found that particular subject beyond my comprehension. My final report card from the Ecole Lavoisier shows a grade in philosophy of 4.5 out of 20, with the remark "very weak in every respect." The teacher's parting words to me were "You will fail the philosophy question on the entrance examination to the Ecole de Physique et de Chimie and you won't get in." I thought: "Go to hell!"

There had been no time to make friends at the Ecole Lavoisier. Every few weeks I called Edith. Sometimes she was already busy, going out with classmates. I tried not to show my disappointment. When we went out, we took the tram or bus to one of the lovely woods surrounding Paris, and had ice cream or some roasted chestnuts for a snack. From time to time Edith sent me a photo of herself with a note disparaging her looks and assuring me of her sincere friendship.

At the beginning of July 1939, I took the three-day entrance examination to the Ecole de Physique et de Chimie. There were about 200 applicants for 40 available places, half of whom would be given to those who had expressed a preference for physics, the other half, for chemistry. When the results were posted outside the school at the end of the month, I pushed my way to the bulletin board and excitedly counted how many intended physicists had higher grades than I. I was number 18 of 20. I was in! I had passed the philosophy question.

Four weeks later, war with Germany was declared. Public notices appeared all over Paris that persons of German nationality between the ages 17 and 55 had to present themselves at a sports stadium in order to be interned. My parents had been exempted from internment by a special order from the Interior Minister for "persons of national importance," but I was not one of those.

For once, I was allowed to take Edith out for dinner and say goodbye to her. I promised to come back for her after the war. I packed the items of food and clothing which had been specified on the notices. From the stadium, buses took us south on a day-long trip to a large army base at Moulins in central France. After a few days, we were transported in groups of about one hundred to smaller camps. I ended up further south at Bourg-Lastic not far from the city Clairemont-Ferrand. Every move was excruciatingly disorganized.

At the camp, we were called "Foreign Workers," but put into barracks within a barbed wire enclosure. Our "work" consisted of being marched every morning and afternoon to a road through a nearby forest. We had to pull out the weeds along the sides of the road and dig drainage channels. A certain distance along the road was prescribed every day or, we were told, our rations of army food would be cut. We asked our guards why we had to do this work. They replied: "This is secret work of national importance." When after a week or so nothing of national importance seemed to occur in the forest, a passive resistance developed and soon the soldiers gave up exhorting and threatening us.

In Paris, my parents had succeeded in having my case examined by a review commission and after three weeks I was liberated from the camp. As soon as I arrived home, I called Edith to give her the good news. School had started again and she, as well as her brother, had lots of homework. Our outings became rare.

I joined my class at the Ecole de Physique et de Chimie and began a period of my life which I count among the happiest. Even though I was the only foreigner, and a German, the other students accepted me fully as their "camerade." Despite the war atmosphere which became more and more pervasive and hysterical, the general feeling in the class was to balance the difficult and demanding studies with as much fun as possible. At lunchtime, several bridge games were going, which I joined as soon as I learned the game.

Already at the beginning of August, before classes had started, there was a get acquainted party in the form of a medieval festival in one of the forests near Paris, at which everybody dressed up. Later in the year, an evening party was organized at a comrade's home, and then an overnight outing in another forest. There were only four girls in our class. When one of the boys wandered off several times with the same girl, I was delegated to tell him that comrades share not only the food, but also the company of the girls. Fifty years later at a class reunion I reminded him of my admonition and he still remembered. Others remembered that in chemistry laboratory, I once brought a pound of sugar, caramelized it on a metal tray over a gas flame, and distributed it, asking other students to distract the instructor with questions about the ongoing experiments.

My March 1940 transcript from the school shows that we took courses not only in mathematics, chemistry and physics, but also in mechanical drawing, metal shop and glass blowing. Metal shop had started with learning how to file down a piece of iron by hand. It took hours and was very tiring. My overall grade point average placed me as eighth out of 39 students. I felt very proud, since I had entered as 35th, and was the youngest in the class.

In early May 1940, public notices appeared once more, for German nationals to report to a large sports stadium on May 15. The papers had talked about the "Fifth Column," the infiltration of Belgian homes by German soldiers dressed up as tourists who then helped the invading forces. Meanwhile northern France had been overrun by the German army, and as an excuse for the second internment the French government hinted that there might be Fifth Columnists in France. The general atmosphere became more hysterical.

I called Edith once more to say goodbye. Holding a bible in my right hand, as she wished in accordance with her Catholic religion, I pledged before God that I would return and get her when the war ended. In subsequent years, if one of my relationships was in danger of becoming too serious, I told my partner about the pledge to Edith. Also, I renewed it in occasional correspondence with her via a friend of mine in Switzerland who forwarded our mail.

Shortly after the end of the war in 1945, after a long pause, I received a letter from Edith saying that she was getting married to a former school friend and that her future husband did not want us to correspond anymore. I was devastated.

In 1947, when I was 25, I had the urge to see England and France again for the first time after the war. I arranged a summer trip to London to visit my brother and, elsewhere, to contact research laboratories with whom I had developed common interests. When I was in Paris, I could not help thinking about Edith. I had often wondered whether her father might have withheld some of my letters from her. I called him up for a meeting. Climbing the same stairs as seven years before, I did not look forward to our conversation. Right away, I asked the father about my suspicion. He gave a vehement denial and I left.

Finally, I could bring this exhausted relationship with Edith to closure, and felt relieved.

7. Roll Call

AS HE DID EVERY DAY after lunch, the sergeant bellowed out the names of the seventy-odd camp inmates. When he called: "MEYERHOF," a voice answered "PRESENT," except it was not mine, but that of my painter friend Max Kainer whom I had asked to answer for me. I was already at the train station in Valence, having taken the bus from the village of Le Cheylard early in the morning. I had escaped by an unguarded gate in the back of the village school where we were interned.

We had arrived in Le Cheylard about a month earlier, on June 22, 1940, after a three-night march from the "Foreign Workers Camp" at Chambaran, eighty miles northeast of Le Cheylard. Officially, we were attached to the 143rd Regional Regiment of the French Army. Our designation was *Prestataires Volontaires*, a phrase one cannot find in a dictionary because it was invented by the French War Ministry to designate foreigners whom they wished to get off the streets in May 1940, but did not consider very dangerous. It can be translated as "Voluntary Toilet Cleaners," except that only rarely was that our duty. Most of the time we were peeling potatoes, and not voluntarily. In any case it represented the lowest rank in the French Army, below that of a private.

Yet, this rank probably saved the lives of some internees, because two days after our arrival at Le Cheylard a delegation of the Kundt Commission came by the camp and demanded to see the list of internees. Kundt Commission delegations visited all French internment camps immediately after the armistice, to take an inventory of all interned Jews, and possibly arrest those on Hitler's enemy list. The delegations had representatives from the German Army, the Nazi Party and the secret police.

Just after the armistice, the Kundt Commission still respected an agreement the French General Weygand had made with his German counterpart, that no members of the French armed forces would be rounded up by the Commission. Probably, because officially we were members of the French Army, no one from our camp was taken away, which released an enormous tension each one of us had felt when the Commission members studied the lists of internees furnished by the camp commander.

℘

The internment was the second one for many of us since the start of the war between Germany and France in September 1939. It had been announced in Paris and throughout France early in May 1940 by notices pasted on walls. The notices asked that all males aged 17 to 65 and all females between 17 and 56, who were citizens of countries governed by German authorities, assemble on May 15 and bring with them a blanket, clothing, and food for a few days. All males in Paris had to assemble in a sports stadium, called Stade de Colombes. I was 18 years old and had to go. My parents were exempt, because my father's biochemical research was classified as important to the national defense.

Soon after my arrival, the Olympic-sized stadium overflowed with internees. After one night, the portable toilets placed on the playing field could no longer be emptied rapidly enough and were simply closed from 8:00 A.M. to 6:00 P.M. People relieved themselves next to the toilets and the stench of the sewage became unbearable. The situation was inhumane.

After a few days, in which one sat or lay on the bleachers or the floorboards of the stadium, lists were posted assigning each person to a bus destined for one of the one hundred internment camps established in France by that time. I was assigned to an army camp at Chambaran. I remember that a soldier hit me in the face because he thought I did not climb into the bus quickly enough. This reminded me of the music teacher in a school in Nazi Germany who had done the same six years earlier, when I had sung incorrectly.

No one on the bus knew where Chambaran was. Later we found out that it was a village in the county Isère, about 300 miles south of Paris, not far from the city of Grenoble. Although supposedly we were volunteers, we were marched into a fenced enclosure within the army camp. In the enclosure, there already were more than a hundred internees. It took about a week until there was sufficient sleeping space and food for the newcomers.

Except for occasional kitchen duty, I do not remember our daily routine, but about a month after our arrival, rumors filtered into the enclosure that the German Army was overrunning France and would soon be in our neighborhood. We became extremely agitated. Finally, the commander of the internees announced he had been told that as a result of the armistice conditions the camp would lie in the zone of France to be occupied by the Germans.

Therefore, the camp would be abandoned and he was ordered to march us beyond the demarcation line into the zone which would not be occupied. The march would take several days. Every one would have to carry whatever he wished to take with him; no transportation of any kind would be furnished by the French army.

I managed to procure a small wheelbarrow to carry my suit-case. I thought in the long run it would be easier on my arms to wheel the suitcase than to carry it. As a physicist I had figured out that by shifting the weight of the suitcase as much forward in the wheelbarrow as possible, most of the weight of the suitcase would be carried by the wheel, despite the additional weight from the wheelbarrow. I offered some space in the wheelbarrow to an older man whose acquaintance I had made, a painter by the name of Max Kainer. I said I would share the space in the wheelbarrow with him for his suitcase, if he would push it half the time, and he agreed.

We were told that we would march only at night, because German fighter planes were strafing roads in France on which they saw moving objects. No lights of any kind were permitted. There would be short rest periods every two hours. When dawn approached, we would be permitted to sleep off the road, preferably in a wooded area so we could not be seen from the air.

During the march, quite a few persons departed to fend for themselves. I talked with Max Kainer about this, but we decided to stay with the main group, because we were unfamiliar with the territory, nor did we know the attitude of the French population if they recognized our German accents. We thought we might well be killed.

On the other hand, I had a constant fear that a German army unit might overtake us. I thought I would end up in a German concentration camp, if I had a document on me which showed I was Jewish. My German passport had a large "J" stamped in it. After a couple of nights of marching and thinking about this, I decided to fling it into the bushes, not foreseeing the difficulties my new "statelessness" would cause me in the future. The identification I had now left consisted of a French identity card for foreigners and my birth certificate.

When after three nights of marching we arrived in the village of Le Cheylard, the commanding officer said we were well beyond the demarcation line, which had become fixed during our march. (Later we heard that the prior camp at Chambaran was also located in the unoccupied zone, so the long march really had been unnecessary. On the other hand, it had the advantage of placing us into a much less restrictive environment.)

The officer went off to negotiate with the mayor of the village. When he returned, we found out he had requisitioned the village school for us. We had to move all the furniture out of the school building and were given straw to sleep on. Over the next few days, conditions improved. I started to explore the school grounds and noticed that only the main entrance to the school was guarded. There was also an unguarded gate in the back, leading to vineyards. As the days passed, I became more daring and went through the gate.

I put into practice some drawing instruction which Max Kainer had been giving me to while the time away. At first, I dared only to walk into the vineyards in the afternoons after the daily roll call, but then I began to venture into the village and the surrounding area to make pencil and ink drawings of what I saw. No one bothered me.

One day, a postcard arrived from my parents. I was puzzled about how they knew where I was. They had arrived in Marseilles toward the end of July and were staying at the Hotel Splendide. They wrote in very guarded terms they were trying to get me out of the camp.

I wrote a note to the camp commander asking whether I could get permission to visit my parents, but when after a few days I didn't hear from him, I took matters into my own hands.

So, now I was sitting in the train to Marseilles, thinking back over the last few weeks. I had missed my parents very much and was longing to see them. I wondered what their reaction would be when I arrived, unannounced.

The Hotel Splendide was next to the train station. When I embraced my parents, I saw they were somewhat upset despite the pleasure of seeing me again after two months. They told me that a forger was preparing a "demobilization" document for me, which would allow me to leave the camp and stay in Marseilles. Without this, I would be arrested if a policeman stopped me, which happened often in Marseilles. But, the document would be ready only in a week or so. There was no alternative; meanwhile I would have to return to the camp.

They told me about their own adventures since we had been separated in Paris in mid-May. They had been unable to get on a train going south from Paris and had to escape from Paris by taxi. Their first destination was Bordeaux, from where they had hoped to reach England. Despite my father's eminence, the British Consul refused to give them a visa which would have allowed them to get onto the last boat to England. Later, I heard that this was one of the very rare occasions in my father's life when he cried.

Returning to Le Cheylard after a couple of days, I was upset and depressed. How could my parents contemplate going to England, and leave me in France, facing an uncertain future? I did not find an answer. And now, what would happen to me when I returned to the camp. Would I be put into prison as an army deserter?

When I saw the camp commander the next day, he said how stupid I had been, because during my absence he had received permission for me to visit my parents for a few days. But now, the permission had expired. He would be willing to apply for me again. This would take some time, though. Meanwhile, I would have to stay in the camp and obey all the rules exactly. At the slightest infraction, I would be incarcerated.

During the next few days, I no longer dared to leave the camp.

To get back into the commander's good graces, I tried to make myself as useful as possible, volunteering for various clean-up and other camp duties.

Finally, a postcard arrived from my parents, hinting that the document they had bought was ready. I asked Max Kainer whether he would be willing to answer the daily roll call for me once more, but he thought that would be too dangerous for him. It took me a couple of days to find someone else who was willing. Out of gratitude, I said I would make a sketch of him. He was very pleased, because no one had ever done that. He was rather poor, and thanked me for all the clothes I was leaving him, as well as other camp goodies and food items I had accumulated. All I put into my pockets for my intended trip back to Marseilles was chocolate.

I told both Max Kainer and my prospective stand-in that, as before, I would take the bus to Valence and from there, the train to Marseilles. But actually, I intended to take a bus all the way to Marseilles. I hoped my story would mislead anyone the camp commander might notify, when in a day or two he discovered that I was missing again.

After an all-day bus trip, I arrived in Marseilles, tired, but happy. Once more, the roll call had given me time to escape.

8. Letters to Varian Fry

Part One

Banyuls-sur-Mer
c/o Madame J. Marill
October, 5, 1940
Dear Mr. Fry,
Although I suppose that you are over[ly] busy, I should like to ask you to send down here my identity card, as soon as you have found it. Perhaps our friend Lé could bring it when he comes [again]? My parents have gone yesterday. Until now they have not come back. With my best wishes,
   Yours truly,
   Walter Meyerhof.

I dropped the letter into the mailbox, heavy hearted that my parents were gone, but glad for them that they would soon be in the U.S. The next day, I sent a telegram to Varian Fry at the Hotel Splendide in Marseille, that my parents had "well passed," meaning that they had succeeded in crossing from the French border town Cerbère into Spain, guided up to the frontier by Léon Ball ("Lé"), a guide who worked for Fry. They had sent me a telegram to let me know.

Now that I was alone at the bed and breakfast (in French, *pension*) of Madame Marill, I had time to recall the past two months. After escaping from the internment camp at LeCheylard, thanks to a forged demobilization paper my parents had bought for me in Marseille, I was able to join my parents in Marseille. Since the end of July they had been staying at the Hotel Splendide, by chance the same hotel where Varian Fry checked in a couple of weeks later, shortly after I had arrived there.

We did not know Varian Fry and were unaware that he had volunteered to the New York based "Emergency Rescue Committee" to help well-known refugees trapped in Vichy France to get out of the country. These were mainly artists, writers, intellectuals and politically active anti-Nazis, whose names were known to the Committee, about two hundred in all.

My father's name was not on Fry's lists, and it is only because of a refugee biochemist who knew his way around, that my father learned about Varian Fry and went to see him in the same hotel where he stayed. My father told Fry that he had been refused an exit visa from France by the Vichy French government, but that he had already asked the President of the Marseille Academy of Sciences to transfer him to a marine biological laboratory in Banyuls-sur-Mer, not far from the Spanish border, hoping to somehow make his way out of France. Fry was only too glad to help a famous Nobel Prize scientist, because he had been urged by his New York committee to assist famous refugees. This would also help with their fund raising. Fry gave my father the name of a French customs officer in the border town Cerbère, who could be bribed to take all three of us to the Spanish frontier.

In Marseille I had felt very uncomfortable with my forged de-mobilization paper. I thought the French military police in Marseille might well have heard about these papers, and after some time would be on the lookout for me because the camp commander would have to report me as a deserter. I urged my father to get us to Banyuls as quickly as possible. We left Marseille at the end of August on a train that took all day.

Within a few days, my father and I visited the customs officer Fry had recommended in the frontier town Cerbère. When he found out that my father was a Nobel Prize scientist, he got cold feet. He said our information must be erroneous; he was not taking anybody to the border. We returned to Banyuls, at a total loss what to do next.

One evening, the bell rang persistently at the front door of our apartment. A young man stood there and said he had heard we wanted to go to Spain and he could help us. I was sure he was an informer for the French secret police and wanted to entrap us. So I replied that we were in Banyuls only because my father did research of importance to the national defense at the marine biological laboratory, and would he please leave us alone. I shut the door before he could say more. After a minute, he knocked loudly. Infuriated, I opened the door and told him I would call the police if he did not leave immediately. He left, but I was shaken by the experience.

Completely unexpectedly, a few days later a German refugee couple stood in front of our door. They introduced themselves as Hans and Lisa Fittko and said Varian Fry had given them our address. They were going to escape to Spain and would be glad to take us along. They had taken refugees with them across other borders, as they managed to make their way from Germany to Czechoslovakia, where Lisa grew up, and from there to Switzerland and finally to France. Although they had just arrived from Marseille, they thought they were experienced enough so that it would not be too difficult for them to find a way into Spain.

My parents must have been a bit skeptical. It was decided that I would go with them, because my Spanish transit visa was expiring in a few days. The next day, the Fittkos and I took off from Banyuls at noon, because then all the border police would be at lunch, a meal never to be missed in France. It was a very sad good-bye for me; I thought I might never see my parents again. The day was Thursday, September 6, 1940. I was 18 years old.

We each carried only an aluminum water bottle and some sandwiches in a bag slung over the shoulder, as if we were going on a hike. The sun was very hot as we made our way along fields and vineyards in a direction the Fittkos thought should lead to Spain. One hill followed the other, and as it became late afternoon, we thought we would finally reach the frontier if we could just make it through the forest up the next hill. We had not stopped to rest and were very tired.

Suddenly, two French border police (*gendarmes*) came out of the woods and asked us what we were doing so close to the frontier. They asked us for identification and saw that we were Germans. Since I spoke better French than the Fittkos, I said we lived in Banyuls and were just hiking. They did not believe me and said they would take us to the police headquarters (*gendarmerie*) in Cerbère. I pleaded with them to let us go, that we were German refugees and wanted to get to Spain to escape from the Gestapo. "You can tell that to our Lieutenant. Come with us and don't try to escape or we will shoot you," they replied.

It took about half an hour to reach the police station. The Lieutenant was completely unsympathetic and said, "We will take you to the court in Perpignan (the main district town) on Saturday. You can tell your story to the judge." We were taken to the prison cells for men and women. There were piles of straw to sleep on. For the evening meal, we were given a bit of black bread and a brown brew they called coffee. We had not eaten since lunchtime.

That night was the one time in my life I prayed to God to save me. I was sure the judge would have us jailed and that eventually I would end up in the hands of the Gestapo.

Around noon the next day, the *gendarmes* took us to a restaurant. Since it was a nice day, we sat outdoors on picnic benches. When I looked around, I recognized the same customs officer with whom my father and I had talked a couple of weeks earlier. He sat at another table, not far from ours. Since we were under guard, I could not go to him, but I suddenly had an idea.

Public toilets in France lacked toilet paper (and still do), so before leaving Banyuls, I had stuffed some into my back pocket. The paper was very stiff, but better than nothing. Turning away from my guard, I wrote on a piece of toilet paper: "Please contact my parents and tell them that we have been jailed in Cerbère. On Saturday, we will be taken before the judge in Perpignan." Our meal was soon over, and when we left, I crumpled up the paper and threw it on the ground, looking at the customs officer and gesturing toward the paper.

On Saturday morning, we were driven to Perpignan. Arriving in the courtroom, I was completely overwhelmed when I saw my parents there. While we were waiting for our turn, they told me that the customs officer had brought them the piece of toilet paper. They immediately went to see the mayor of Banyuls. He phoned the judge whom he knew well (both had been members of the Socialist Party) and told him our story.

When our case came up, a *gendarme* explained that the Fittkos and I had been caught close to the border, trying to leave France illegally, without exit visas. The judge then said to the *gendarme*, "Thank you for your presentation" and turning to us, "You are free to go." It was unbelievable.

❡

Fifty years later, Lisa Fittko told me she had completely forgotten this episode, and it is not in her book *Mein Weg über die Pyreneen* (*My Way Across the Pyrenees*), published in 1985. I am sure I did not imagine it, because I have a letter dated September 22, 1940, returned by a Swiss friend with whom I corresponded regularly. I had written, "Some time ago, through an unfortunate incident, I was forced to spend three nights in a *gendarmerie* prison." I did not write more; I was afraid of the censor.

Part Two

The next half year was the most complicated period of my life. Although I remember little, I am relatively well informed, because my mother saved most of my letters, as well as copies of correspondence between my father and others who tried to help me and finally succeeded in getting me out of France and to the U.S. These were, besides the Emergency Rescue Committee, the Unitarian Service Committee, which had offices in Marseille and Lisbon, the American Friends Service Committee, whose offices were in Perpignan and in Marseille, and the Lisbon office of the Rockefeller Foundation, which was paying one-half of my father's salary in the U.S. as well as the trips across the ocean for the family. Also, I have copies of correspondence between Varian Fry and myself during this half year, of which the originals are in the exile archives of a German library in Frankfurt (Die Deutsche Bibliothek).

There is no doubt in my mind that all the help I received I owe to the fact that I was the son of a famous Nobel-Prize scientist. To my sister who was studying medicine at Johns Hopkins University, I wrote at the end of 1940: "Father's ghost is opening all doors for me."

§

Before leaving Banyuls, my parents had arranged for my lodging at a bed and breakfast (*pension*). I wrote to them that the landlady, Madame Marrill, was really spoiling me. She had given me the downstairs guestroom, the best in the house. Although she was supposed to provide only breakfast, and food was rationed, she also cooked for me in the evening for a very modest fee.

During the day, I kept busy by studying a book on Mechanics which I had carried with me all the way from Paris. In the afternoon, I went to the beach which was only a couple of blocks from the pension, and had a swim in the Mediterranean.

Two or three times a week, I visited the Fittkos, who had settled in an apartment located directly over the Banyuls Customs Office. Without ever asking what they were doing, I tried to be helpful to them with personal errands. Later, I found out that they were bringing refugees sent by Fry to the border. They never had any mishap since the one with me.

In the winter, Lisa Fittko came down with jaundice. She developed a high fever and one evening finally sent me to get a doctor. I went to the doctor on duty at that hour. I explained to him that Lisa was very sick with jaundice and could he please prescribe some medication or perhaps also see her. On my own, I mentioned that the Fittkos were German refugees, but that he would be fully paid for his service. Then he said; "I do not treat German refugees," and sent me away. I returned to the Fittkos. They were very upset by what had happened and thought it was my fault. I felt terribly bad, but hurried to the village pharmacy and got some medication suggested by the pharmacist, which in the next few weeks cured the jaundice.

A year ago, I revisited Banyuls for the first time and met a longtime resident. He told me that that doctor was well known in the village for being the only Nazi sympathizer among the doctors, and that at the end of the war he had to flee, because the villagers were going to kill him.

In the *pension*, I started chatting with an elderly English lady who had retired to France twenty years earlier and was the only other guest. We went for walks in the surroundings. I called her Eldy, because the initials of her name were L. D. Also, she was elderly. To my parents I wrote that she was 90 years old, but I think now that she must have been between 70 and 80. She called me Boris, because I reminded her of the mythological Russian Boris Gudenov who in 1519 supposedly arranged the murder of the newborn child of Ivan the Terrible. I did not quite understand my connection with him.

When the weather turned rainy and cold, and we did not go out, Eldy tried to broaden my horizons by interesting me in English literature, giving me books to read which she had. This was a somewhat hopeless undertaking, but I did enjoy reading the books and my physics studies lessened.

At the end of October, I wrote to Varian Fry that I had applied for permission to travel to Marseille in order to inquire at the U.S. consulate about the status of my American visa. When after more than a month I had not heard from the *Préfecture*, I assumed the permission had been denied.

In November, my lost French identity card was located in the files of the U.S. consulate, which was understaffed and disorganized, and Fry mailed it to me. Since it expired just a few days later, I went to the *Préfecture* at Perpignan and asked to see the head of the administrative office. I explained my status to him and then asked him, "Don't you have to arrest me because I came without a travel permit?" and he replied, "That's not my job, that's the job of the police."

To help me with all my difficulties, Fry sent one of his coworkers, Maurice Rivière, to visit me. It turned out to be the same man in whose face I had shut our door a month earlier. His true name was Marcel Verzeano, a Rumanian doctor who assisted Fry's clients suffering from physical or mental stress. At the same time, he was setting up an underground railroad to guide Fry's most endangered refugees through Spain.

At the beginning of every month, I went to the office of the American Service Committee in Perpignan and picked up a monthly allowance. My father paid $50 to their New York office, and I was given 2500 French Francs, thereby bypassing the currency exchange restrictions.

On November 20, I received a telegram from Dr. Charles Joy, the head of the Marseille and Lisbon offices of the Unitarian Service Committee, urging me come to Marseille. He was leaving France, but before leaving wanted to help me with the U.S. immigration visa, possibly without the requirement of having to present a French exit visa. I was very excited and immediately wrote to my parents that I would go to Marseille the same evening. In view of the urgency, I decided to risk the trip, even though my identity card had not yet been renewed and I lacked the necessary travel permit.

To avoid encountering a police patrol, I took the latest night train. There was one change, in the town of Narbonne. I waited in the third class toilet and came out only at the last minute to catch the connection to Marseille. To bypass the police checkpoint at the Marseille station exit, I looked for the one and only toilet which could be reached from a station platform. I had been told that the same toilet also served the station restaurant, and that one could leave from there through the restaurant without being checked.

Dr. Joy later reported to his head office in Boston:

…Before I left [France], I wired Walter to come to Marseille. He came without his *carte d'indentité*, and no other papers of any sort. There is a way of getting out of the Gare St. Charles at Marseille without passing through the usual control, so he came right to the Hotel Terminus where I was staying. He had no papers, so he could not stay at a hotel. We arranged, however, to have him kept for three nights in a private house, and told him what streets to avoid in Marseille, and other places, where he must not run the risk of being stopped to show his papers.

I took him to the American Consulate, and was delighted to find that he would be able to get his American visa as soon as a German [quota] number was available, which would be in about two months the consul thought. Since then, the German quota has been thrown open, so he should have it immediately, provided he can get a *visa de sortie* (exit visa). Walter thought he could manage that, as he has some good connections at the local *Préfecture.*

Then the problem would be his Spanish visa, which at the moment looks insuperable, but we are always working on other ways of getting out of France, and there may be a chance. In short, Walter, at the moment is safe and has an even chance of getting away. When I go back to France, if I do, another step may be open. Is any money available for his transportation and other expenses?"

The family where I was put up for three nights was a family of Polish refugees with two children, living in a tiny apartment. I slept on the floor. They had a son my age, who in the U.S. became one of my best friends.

Before I returned to Banyuls, Dr. Joy gave me 5000 Francs for later expenses, in case he would not return to France. My father repaid the Unitarian Service Committee in Boston with a $100 check.

In Banyuls, I started collecting the documents I would need for the French exit visa application. I handed it in on December 4.

I wrote to my sister that I was so distracted by all this that I could not concentrate on physics and that I was looking forward to getting back to the discipline of studying sometime in the future.

In mid-December, I got a letter from the U.S. Consulate in Marseille, telling me that they had received a telegram from the State Department asking me to come to Marseille as soon as I could. They did not say what the telegram was about, and I was in a quandary what to do, because I had to travel again without a permit and did not have the French exit visa which I thought was required for the issuance of the U.S. immigration visa.

I decided to first spend Christmas at the pension. Madame Marill roasted a large bird, with chestnuts on the side, and a flan for dessert. On the 25th, I took the night train to Marseille and went to the American consulate the next day. I reported to my parents:

> …I heard from [Vice Consul] Bingham that I could have my immigration visa. He first said 'I suppose if you have no *visa de sortie* it is no use giving you a visa.' I nearly exploded, but that would have been no use, and everything had come out wonderfully now. There was a telegram about me from [Secretary of State] Cordell Hull, that's why the visa was issued. I got it on January 2nd.

Since my identity card had meanwhile been renewed, I could stay at a hotel, but on the weekend Fry took me to his country house retreat, "Villa Air-Bel." Several artists, writers and other intellectuals were housed there while they waited for their visas. Most were surrealists, among them André Breton and Max Ernst. At dinner they laughed and flirted with their girlfriends and they organized races of praying mantis insects on the tablecloth, which they had stored in small bottles. I was 18 years old and felt very uncomfortable among the grownups and their antics, so as soon as the meal was over, I went to my room and shut the door. Nowadays, I am often asked whether I ever met the famous artists at the Villa Air-Bel, and I have to confess that I missed the chance of a lifetime.

During that week in Marseille, coming out of a restaurant, I ran into Max Kainer, the painter friend from my last internment camp. Although during our time in the camp he was very negative about the USA and I was so much under his influence that for a while I told my parents I would never go to the USA, now he asked whether my father could use his connections to help him get to the States. Kainer mentioned that he had worked in Hollywood for the Ziegfield Follies, and in Paris had designed the decorations for *Entente Cordiale*, a famous film about the First World War.

Before leaving Marseille, I was able to renew my Portuguese transit visa, and then returned to Banyuls. I telegraphed my parents that I hoped to see them soon. I wrote to the representative of the Rockefeller Foundation to please reserve space on a boat for me, leaving Lisbon around mid-February.

Banyuls-sur-Mer
January 30, 1941.
     Dear Mr. Fry,
     In addition to the American and Portuguese visa which I already possess, I have now been granted the French exit visa by the Préfecture in Perpignan.
     Three weeks ago I made a first Spanish visa application and two weeks later the visa was refused to me. Yesterday, I made a second application at the consulate in Perpignan.
     Have you heard of any boat going between Marseille and Lisbon, because I could use that now?
     I am very sincerely yours,
     W.E. Meyerhof

Part Three

The bulk of the correspondence in my files from January and February 1941 is about my Spanish transit visa. Since November of the previous year, Spain had instituted a new requirement that visas be entered only on valid passports. But, I had thrown my German passport into the bushes during the flight into the unoccupied zone of France half a year earlier. In addition, special permission now had to be obtained from the Foreign Ministry in Madrid for any person of military age to cross Spain. In 1941 Franco still dealt very gingerly with Hitler because it looked as if Germany might be victorious in the war. German and other refugees from countries occupied by Germany often were denied entry into Spain. The rejections were arbitrary and depended on the particular border officer one encountered. I urged my parents to ask the State Department to contact the Spanish Foreign Ministry and Varian Fry to use his influence, in order to obtain the special permission for me.

While waiting around in Banyuls, the weather had turned nice and I decided to participate in a wine-making ceremony, called *vindage*, for the Banyuls aperitif wine.

As did other young people, I climbed into a barrel filled with grapes, together with a girl from the village. Grabbing hold of each other, we tried to steady each other and to balance ourselves on the slippery surface. A band played music to which we sang *vindage* songs and danced with naked feet, thereby crushing the grapes. At the end of the day, we were paid a small amount. The *vindage* went on for a week, but many volunteers dropped out earlier because their feet started bleeding. I did not wait for that to happen to me.

When my second Spanish visa application was refused in mid-February, I became desperate and decided to go to Marseille in order to explore other possible routes of getting out of France, such as going to Lisbon directly by boat, or via Casablanca, or even via Brazil. Fry helped me to explore some of these possibilities. After a week, I knew that nothing would develop quickly, so I moved to cheaper lodging and wrote to Madame Marill that I was giving up my room in her pension, hoping she could store my belongings until my return.

I rented a room under the roof of a hotel, without electricity or running water, in which one easily hit one's head on the ceiling with the slightest upward movement. The only way I could stand up straight was to stick my head out of a small skylight which provided illumination during the day and a nice view of Marseille rooftops. At night, I lit a candle. The room cost 10 Francs (20 U.S. cents) a day. Dinner at a restaurant cost about the same, but to fill my stomach, I munched biscuits and nougat in my room, which were cheap. Fortunately, from time to time friends of my parents, Varian Fry, Dr. Joy, or the Head of the Quaker committee took me out for a meal.

Since Fry already had an office boy, I offered Dr. Joy to work as an errand boy for him. He had returned from his Lisbon office at the beginning of March. My first task was to find more office space for the Unitarian Service Committee office, and after a couple of weeks I succeeded in finding a suitable place. Another time, after a lot of searching, I was able to locate a store selling picks and shovels, which Dr. Joy wanted to distribute in internment camps for digging water runoffs from outdoor showers.

Toward the end of March, perhaps by bribing a functionary at the Spanish consulate in Marseille, Dr. Joy arranged to have instructions sent to the Spanish consular branch in Perpignan to issue issue me a transit visa, stamped into the "Affidavit in lieu of Passport" from the U.S. Consulate instead of a regular passport. I immediately returned to Perpignan and obtained a visa valid for entering Spain through the border towns Port Bou or Le Perthus. The visa, issued on March 25, was valid for ten days.

The next morning, I cabled my parents "Starting Lisbon tomorrow cheerfully Meyerhof." From the Banque de France, I applied for permission to take money out of France and obtained 3000 French Francs and 40 U.S. dollars, using the 5000 Francs from Dr. Joy, which I had deposited.

I did not want to leave France through Cerbère and enter Spain through the closest town, Port Bou, because recently refugees had been rejected there. Dr. Joy agreed that it might be safer to enter through Le Perthus, which is in the middle of the Pyrenees and was rarely used by refugees.

Early in the morning of March 27 I said goodbye to Madame Marill and Eldy and took the train and then the bus to Le Perthus. I arrived shortly after noon. With the exit visa in hand, I had no difficulty passing through the French border post. After dragging my suitcase in the hot sun to the Spanish border station half an hour away, the officer there looked at my "Affidavit in lieu of Passport" with suspicion and told me to wait because he had to check with Madrid. I pointed out as politely as I could that my Spanish transit visa was valid for entry through Le Perthus, but he insisted that he would have to check with Madrid first. I was apprehensive, but powerless against his arbitrary decision.

After waiting for five hours, I was told I would not be admitted into Spain; I would have to return to France. It was devastating news. I had tried everything, and now would certainly not survive. I was readmitted into France, and late at night arrived in Banyuls. I had to wake up Madame Marill, and asked her whether she could put me up again. She graciously agreed.

The next day, I cabled Dr. Joy. He cabled back that in two days he was going to Lisbon and he would try to take me along as his official secretary. I should meet him on the train to Cerbère, which would make a brief stop at Banyuls. When I boarded the train, I told Dr. Joy I still had about 2000 French Francs and 40 dollars on me. He asked me to give him the dollars. With his own money, he bought tickets to Barcelona from the Thomas Cooks Wagonlits agent in Port Bou. Then he pressed the 40 dollars into the agent's hand and asked him to see to it that the Spanish border police would not make any difficulty for his secretary—and they did not. I could not hide my relief. My odyssey had come to an end.

We stayed overnight in Barcelona. Dr. Joy wanted to stop in Madrid for a day of sightseeing. He was interested mainly in seeing the destruction inflicted during the Spanish Civil War with the help of the Luftwaffe on the university and its students who had resisted the establishment of the Franco dictatorship.

We arrived in Lisbon on April 2. In a birthday letter to my father on April 12, I told him how I was spending my days in Lisbon, waiting to find space on a boat to the U.S. I described in great detail what efforts I had made to stand in line for hours at the offices of various shipping companies, and how I had narrowly missed one third-class opening. At the same time, the representative of the Rockefeller Foundation used his connections to find a berth. He asked me to check with him every day.

In Dr. Joy's office, I met a young man my age and his sister who worked there. I had befriended him at the Camp de Chambaran where we had been interned. In Lisbon, he and I visited various art galleries and museums. (He later became a well-known painter in New York, but died shortly after he had his first exhibition.) In the evenings, I often took out his sister. When I mailed the letter to my father on April 17, I did not tell him that three days earlier, the Rockefeller Foundation had found space for me on a boat leaving the next day. But, I had neglected to check in with them that day, because I was on an all-day outing into the countryside around Lisbon with the sister. The representative was furious.

Now, the situation became critical, because my U.S. immigration visa was going to expire on May 2, which meant I would have to be on a boat by then, or the whole visa application procedure would need to be repeated, taking months. On April 27, the Rockefeller representative located another berth for me on a Portuguese cargo ship.

Lisbon

April 28, 1941

Dear Mr. Fry,

Before leaving the continent in two days time on a Portuguese cargo boat, I want to send you a small word for the great help and kindness you showed to me always. Everything turned out so well for me in the end, and I am sure you were not the least who pushed my luck in that direction. I have heard that you have some small troubles, but I hope that is nothing, and that we may meet soon in the USA.

Please remember me to Mr. and Mrs. Bénédite, Mr. and Mrs. Bohne, Jean and all the others who know me.

Very sincerely yours,

Walter Meyerhof

Some time after I had arrived in the U.S., Eldy wrote to me: "Before I left Banyuls, the Gestapo came looking for you."

9. Banana Split

"A FRIED EGG SANDWICH, please, and a small glass of apple juice," I said to Mrs. Cohen, who together with her husband ran Cohen's Luncheonette near the campus of the University of Pennsylvania in Philadelphia. I paid twenty-two cents and picked up my plate. My eyes passed the counter, where I saw the strangest dish ever. On a curved oblong glass plate a banana had been split lengthwise in half, with two vanilla ice cream balls, some whipped cream and ground nuts, a dab of chocolate sauce and two cookies sticking out. I thought, that must be a counter decoration. In Europe, no one could possibly eat fruit and ice cream together, and with chocolate sauce, too, without getting violently ill. Since nobody touched the dish, I thought it must be made out of plastic. The next day, though, a woman student actually picked up the dish and took it to her table. I thought, "Americans are peculiar people. They eat fruit, ice cream and chocolate together and don't mind becoming sick." Later in the week, I finally dared to ask and was told that the dish tastes very good. It was called Banana Split. I remained skeptical.

I had just arrived from France. My parents had met my boat in New York when it docked in mid-May 1941 after a two-week zigzag trip from Lisbon to avoid U-boats. (It was sunk a year later.) It was a small freighter which had staterooms for eight passengers.

My parents took me to their apartment in Philadelphia. I wanted to enroll at the University of Pennsylvania, where, as the child of a university professor, I could go tuition free, if I was academically qualified. My goal was to get a Ph.D. in Physics, but I was told I had to make up undergraduate deficiencies for a year before I would be considered for graduate studies. Even before that I had to pass two consecutive summer courses in beginning English composition and in English literature.

Although I found the literature course easy because I had studied most of the works at Dulwich College in London, I disliked English grammar and had the greatest difficulty writing compositions about my life every week. My experiences in France were too recent, and I really wanted to forget them. The teacher told us it helps to write a composition if one works together with someone and then criticizes each other's work. Since I did not know anybody in the class, I was at a loss.

To be less distracted than at home where my mother puttered around, I went to the library study room to do my homework. Several times I saw a woman in her early twenties at another table. She was also in my class. One day, as she was leaving the room, I approached her and asked whether she would like to be my study partner. "Yes," she said, "that would be nice. I am also a stranger in Philadelphia." She told me she was taking summer courses as part of a teaching credential for her hometown school in central Pennsylvania.

The first few days, we sat on campus benches, but when my parents left for the summer to go to Woods Hole where my father had been given an office in the Marine Biological Laboratory, I offered some quiet space in our apartment. We agreed that we would work in separate rooms on our compositions for an hour and a half and then critique each other's work, before having a drink and going our separate ways.

As soon as I could, I introduced myself to the Chairman of the Physics Department. He was an older man and very friendly. I told him about my plans and asked whether there might be some part-time work to keep me involved in physics and busy during the summer.

I explained to him the practical training I had had in Paris. He asked whether I could solder. I said yes, and he took me to his laboratory. He showed me a piece of apparatus and told me he would be very happy if over the summer I could get it working. Apparently, a graduate student had abandoned it unfinished. He mentioned that there was no money to pay me since he had not counted on employing me, but that in the fall there might be a small monthly subsidy. I did not mind; I mainly wanted to learn, and my parents had been giving me pocket money for food. I showed up in the lab whenever I did not have classes or homework.

One day, my study partner told me that she was contemplating the engagement to a man from her hometown. A wedding had even been tentatively planned for the fall. He was a scientist in his early thirties who had heard of my father's work and would be fascinated to meet him. Then she continued, "You see, he is impotent and he wanted me to go to Philadelphia to have a last fling, and to decide whether I really want to get engaged to him." I had never heard that word before and, after a while, asked whether he had a mental affliction. I knew about those, and felt very sympathetic. No, she said, the condition was not mental, but due to an accident in his youth.

My 19 years of life had not prepared me for being the object of a fling, especially under such peculiar conditions. The idea frightened and intrigued me and I tried not to think about it, even though we continued to meet for study sessions. Finally, one Saturday I invited her to a candlelight dinner at home, trying to imitate one of the dishes I had gleaned from my mother. On the following Saturday, we organized a small evening potluck party with some friends she had made, and danced and sang into the night. I remembered that the apartment lease stated the walls were soundproof.

I reported my activities in weekly letters to my parents, which my mother kept and I could reread 60 years later. Although I do not have my parents' responses, evidently they were very tolerant in letting me lead the kind of life I chose.

After a lot of wavering, in mid-summer, my study partner decided to go through with the engagement, but we continued our study sessions for the remainder of the six-week summer quarter term. Her fiancé came to visit occasionally. I wondered how he felt about me, but we never touched on the subject and only talked about our mutual scientific interests.

I was invited to the wedding in the fall. A year later a girl was born and they urged me to visit them in Baltimore. When I arrived, they asked me to be their daughter's godfather. I did not know what that meant. After they explained, I said I was only twenty years old and would have too many obligations as a graduate student. But they insisted, and since the baby looked very sweet, I agreed. At first, each year I sent the daughter a birthday card, but then my communications became less and less frequent. I never saw her again and after 21 years decided she could now go through life on her own. I had not been a good godfather.

After the summer of 1941, I needed to get away from the complexities of human involvement and concentrated on my studies and lab work, well past midnight and on weekends. After a few months, though, I felt weary and I longed for some personal contact. As part of my make-up program, I had to take a class in social studies. I began talking with a young woman of my age. She told me she had just broken off an engagement and needed to recover from the experience, but she was willing to have a cup of coffee with me once in a while. She came from a well-to-do suburban Philadelphia family who had a farm with horses. Her main hobbies were riding and reading and writing poetry and she showed me some of her own poems. In the middle of the summer we went on a week's bicycle trip to some nearby youth hostels. She was very pleasant, but over the six months we had known each other, she always held herself aloof and after that summer, we separated.

When the new school year opened that fall, Cohen's Luncheonette was in full swing again. Prices had gone up; a fried egg sandwich with apple juice now cost thirty cents. One day, I heard behind me a couple of young women talking in a strange language. Not being able to control my curiosity, I asked them whether they were conversing in Norwegian. One of the women said, "No, it's Bulgarian." She introduced the other woman as her sister and continued, "As a matter of fact, I know who you are, and I work for your father." I was completely taken aback and thought she must be joking. But, then I remembered that a few days earlier I had visited my father's laboratory, and he had introduced me to his new assistant, a young woman in a white lab coat. She seemed to be in her early thirties and I had paid no attention to her.

That changed over the next six months. She was nine years older than I and mature enough to let me grow in the next three years toward adulthood without making any personal demands. We both enjoyed our relationship, except for our political ideas.

Her country had a long-standing historical bond with Russia and was controlled by communists. She believed that all countries, including the U.S., needed to go through a communist stage in order to attain social justice for its people. I could not condone the killings by either Stalin or by Hitler, but she saw that as a price which had to be paid for the eventual beneficial result.

We decided to avoid discussions about politics. Since I was unfamiliar with American history, I agreed after some hesitancy to attend with her an evening course on history from a Marxist viewpoint, sponsored by a group calling itself the United People's Action Committee, which tried to bring whites and blacks together. I was careful never to identify myself, since I had applied for an FBI security clearance to be employed in war-related work in the Physics Department. In the history course, the subject of slavery interested me most. In my childhood days in Heidelberg I had always empathized with beggars coming to our house and more generally with the disadvantaged ever since.

At the end of June 1944, my mother called in the middle of the night from Woods Hole, where my parents were spending the summer again. My father had had a heart attack after a tennis game. Fortunately, a New York doctor, one of their best friends, was also in Woods Hole and was immediately called. He could give an injection in time, to calm the heart. My father was now resting in a local hospital. He was not allowed to move any part of his body or speak any word, just blink with his eyes.

I wanted to come to Woods Hole right away to help my mother. She said she would first have to ask the doctor. Besides, two years earlier I had been classified as an alien and had to get permission to travel out of Philadelphia at the downtown office of the United States Attorney. We agreed that as soon as permission was granted, I should call my mother again and check whether the doctor would allow me to visit my father, but in any case I would not be able to see him longer than a few minutes.

It took a day before the gravity of the situation became clear

to me and brought frightening thoughts. I found it difficult to concentrate on my studies and research which I had meanwhile started. Would I be able to take over as the man of the house? Would I
have to stop working toward a Ph.D. and try to find a job to support my mother and myself? Of course, my brother and sister
would contribute, but would I be sufficiently qualified and earn
enough? And, would I be mature enough to cope?

When I saw my father a few days later, I took hold of his hand
as gently as I could. I told him about my work, how I was involved
in war work connected with radar detection. My father smiled
weakly, signaling his approval. His assistant wanted me to let him
know that she was willing to do anything he wanted, including
typing letters, which had not been part of her job. There was no
need for him to continue paying a secretary.

Since it was uncertain how long my father's recovery would
take, my mother asked me to look for a ground floor apartment in
Philadelphia for the three of us, which did not have any steps. Because it was summer, the search was not too difficult, and I arranged the entire move. I was glad I could contribute in some way.

At the end of the summer, my father was transported to
Mount Sinai Hospital in New York, so that his doctor friend could
continue caring for him. He had several minor heart attacks and in
the end had to stay in the hospital more than ten months. My
mother had found lodging in New York and kept him company
every day. I visited them several times and was happy to see him
improve slowly. But, when he finally returned to Philadelphia, he
looked much older.

In summer 1946, my father's assistant decided to return to
Bulgaria. She became a translator and remained single. We stayed
in annual contact until she died.

I also left for my first physics job at the University of Illinois in
Urbana. I was content with my inner self and the accomplishment

of having acquired a Ph.D. in Physics, at the age of 24. The same year, I became a naturalized American citizen. After the swearing-in ceremony, I asked myself what should be my first act as an American. I decided to have a Banana Split. It tasted very good.

10. Interlude

SUDDENLY I HEARD HER SAY, "I love you." I was sure I had misunderstood, so I asked whether she could please repeat what she had just told me. She said, "I am in love with you," with an air of defiance, vulnerability and relief. I did not want to hurt her, so I answered, "I also have affectionate feelings for you, but I need some time before I can really respond." I tried to steer the conversation back to the purpose of our afternoon meeting.

We sat across from each other in a coffee shop near the campus of the University of Illinois in Urbana. We had arranged to get together for half an hour in order to discuss the cheapest and most convenient way to travel to the town where a meeting had been called to coordinate statewide the actions of the many small groups in Illinois supporting Henry Wallace's Progressive Party. We had agreed to be part of the delegation from the Urbana group, mainly to try to prevent extreme leftists from taking important positions in the party. We decided that the best transportation would be provided by Greyhound bus. After parting, I returned to my work at the Physics Department, completely preoccupied by what she had just said, oblivious to the snow piled everywhere.

It was 1946. I was 24. At the beginning of September, I had arrived in Urbana. Searching in the local paper, I had easily found a room because most students had not yet arrived. The next day, I introduced myself to the chairman of the Physics Department, who had offered me a two-year position as Research Assistant Professor at a monthly salary of $300, five times as much as my previous graduate student stipend.

In applying for the position, I had indicated that I wanted to learn nuclear physics in order to use its techniques in the further study of surfaces of solids, the subject of my recently completed doctor's thesis. The chairman suggested I visit the various nuclear physics groups in the Department and then decide which one I would like to join. Also, he mentioned there were openings in the teaching program, but I told him I really wanted to concentrate first on learning a new field of physics. I would be glad to consider teaching later.

I knew that research productivity counted most in an academic career, so I chose a group which I thought would allow me the most rapid advancement. The group was headed by a husband and wife, both Professors in the Department and both highly recognized nuclear physicists. The husband was more interested in generating ideas, and his wife was more involved in experimentation, so I agreed to work with her, hoping soon to generate my own ideas and pursue my own interests.

In the mornings, I went to the departmental library and read textbooks and research articles about nuclear physics or I sat in on advanced courses which had not been offered at the University of Pennsylvania. In the afternoons I was in the laboratory, assisting a graduate student supervised by the wife, but after a few months I began to make suggestions. Every evening after dinner, our supervisor came to the lab and asked what we had accomplished during the day and proposed what should be done that night. She did not consider that we might wish to sleep, and showed her disappointment when the following time we reported that we had not been able to do all she had proposed.

Although at first I was pleased by the conscientious attention given to my progress, after half a year I expressed a desire for more independence. I was given the opportunity to assemble my own experimental apparatus, and scrounged around in other labs for equipment parts I could use. After some time, I supervised a graduate student.

For lunch I usually brought a sandwich to the lab, which I had made in my landlady's kitchen in order to save money. Once a week, I joined other professional Research Associates and visitors in the group for lunch. Most were close to my age. All were male, and some conversations reminded me of the dorm talk at Dulwich College in London a decade earlier.

I heard that during the academic year, a professor and his wife had Open House every Saturday, to which any physics or mathematics graduate student could come for company and a dinner snack. All one had to do is to call up the day before, so that enough food would be available. Since the Open House was meant for graduate students, I felt it did not apply to me, even though my lunch companions, all of whom had Ph.D. degrees, did not hesitate to go there.

Instead, on Saturdays, when I felt somewhat lonely, I attended mixers for graduate or even undergraduate students, at which a dance orchestra played. I looked young enough to pass for a graduate student, and made up stories about what I was doing at the university. Using dancing steps I had learned in Paris seven years earlier, I succeeded in keeping most of my partners happy, at least the younger ones.

One Saturday, one of my lunch group participants called me up and urged me to simply come along to the Open House. He said I shouldn't be so moralistic, and that there was always more than enough food. Since I had no plans for the evening, I went along, with somewhat of a bad conscience. The host and hostess were very welcoming, saying they had heard about me and were very pleased to have me. About a dozen students and others were standing or sitting around. I mainly listened and did not say much.

The husband was in his early fifties and the wife in her mid-thirties. They had two small children, a boy about four and a girl about six years old. Between 6:00 and 7:00 P.M., dishes were put out on a table and everybody was told to help themselves.

The conversation was dominated by the husband and soon turned to politics. It became clear that they were both very liberal-ly oriented and that the wife was a committed admirer of Henry Wallace, whereas the husband had a more distant intellectual point of view. Most of the students were quiet and ate.

Around 9:00 P.M. everybody started leaving. I took some dish-es into the kitchen and offered to help with washing up. I said it was the least I could do to thank them for welcoming me as a non-graduate student and for coming unannounced. The wife agreed to let me dry.

From then on, I showed up every two or three weeks at the Open House. I started playing with the children and sometimes brought them little toys as an indirect thank-you present. Occa-sionally, I was invited during the week when the wife asked me to accompany her to a discussion group interested in the Progressive Party. In the local newspaper, I had read speeches Henry Wallace had given and felt in sympathy with his ideas about social justice. In early December, the discussion group was asked to send half a dozen delegates to a state meeting set for the following spring.

When I met the wife again after our meeting in the café to

plan our trip, I explained to her that I liked her and her husband very much, but wanted to avoid the kind of emotional situation I had experienced six years earlier, when I had been entangled in a triangular relationship. I needed time to develop my feelings towards her without pressure. She said she could wait, and that her husband would never find out because her behavior toward him would remain unchanged. I was somewhat skeptical that her husband would not sense some subtle change in her.

I went home to Philadelphia for Christmas. I told my parents that I had plans to visit Europe during the coming summer. I had recently become an American citizen and no longer needed to worry about the complicated readmission procedures for aliens traveling abroad. My salary was sufficient to save the $1,500 which I had estimated for the trip. In addition, I could continue the monthly $25 payments I had made to my parents to recompense them partially for their subsidy of my graduate education.

On the trip, I wanted to spend July in England, where my brother and his wife had offered me a mattress on the floor in their tiny apartment in London, and August on the continent. I thought that in addition to seeing friends and places to which I had become attached seven years earlier, I would visit half a dozen nuclear physics laboratories in whose research programs I had become interested. Since I had hardly published anything myself, I would offer to give lectures on the general research program of our group, hoping to receive a small subsidy for travel expenses. My parents expressed their general approval and I returned to Urbana feeling more confident.

In early spring, the wife and I took a bus to the three-day state meeting of the Progressive Party. We were both booked into the meeting hotel where rooms were available at reduced prices.

The meeting was like a mini-convention. Previously prepared resolutions were proposed by the Steering Committee chair. Five to ten minutes were given for discussion within each delegation. Each delegation chair would then report a yes or no vote or an amendment to the resolution. Most amendments were turned down by the Steering Committee. Since each day the meeting stretched late into the night, by the third day when the most important resolutions were proposed, the delegates turned up late and were exhausted. The whole experience gave me a taste of democracy in action and an understanding of national conventions. I developed mixed feelings.

On the return bus trip to Urbana, I gently squeezed her hand.

As the summer of 1947 approached, I was increasingly occupied with organizing my European trip. I had booked for the end of June a trip on a converted troop ship, on which one could make the ten-day New York–Southampton trip in dormitory accommodation for $117 one way. By mid-May, I had received positive replies from nearly all the laboratories I wanted to visit, and half had offered me small travel subsidies.

At the beginning of June, the husband and wife were leaving Urbana with their children to go on holiday. Her parting words to me were: "Don't do anything foolish in Europe."

My brother and his wife fetched me from the boat train in London. I had not seen him for a decade. I had not met his wife before because they had just married. She was very friendly.

An hour after we arrived at their apartment, the doorbell rang. There stood Miriam. She said she was just on her way home from supervising a small group of preschool children and wanted to drop by before going home, but I think she had been unable to contain her curiosity about me. We had last met nine years earlier in Berlin when she had called me a "dumb ape" in response to my asking her to go out with me. Now, I was struck by her beautiful smile and easy laughter. Unpacking, I handed her some chocolate and nylon stockings I had brought along as general gifts. She accepted both gladly, because they were unobtainable in post-war London. When she was about to leave, I asked whether we could meet again in a couple of days after I had had rested up from the trip. This time she agreed.

We walked to a park and talked without end, telling each other about our lives since the Berlin days. We felt very much at ease; we had known each other since our childhood days. She told me that for the past six months, she had been supervising each weekday morning and early afternoon four to six children whose mothers were working. During the war years, she had been one of a dozen aides employed by Anna Freud to care for children whose parents were not at home during the day, because they were in the army or working in factories.

There was not enough time that day, so we arranged another rendezvous. After a week, I took her hand and she did not withdraw it. The next day, I had to leave for my first laboratory visit in Birmingham and in the evening I phoned her and we spoke for an hour. The following week, I had to be in Oxford and I invited her to come along just for fun. She accepted.

I took her on a punting trip on the shallow river Isis which traverses Oxford. I had never punted before and had to learn how to push the flat-bottomed boat along by standing up and poking a long wooden stick into the muddy bottom of the river. Holding the punting rod with both hands spread apart, at first the free end of the rod would either keep floating in the water when I tried to push it in or it got stuck in mud, so I nearly fell in. Watching other punters, over the course of the afternoon I slowly learned how to thrust the rod correctly by letting it slide on the square end of the boat, but I was exhausted and sat down next to Miriam. I took her hand and asked her to marry me and she said yes. It had been three weeks since my arrival in London.

Miriam immediately phoned her mother, with whom she had

been living, and she was very happy. When I called my parents, they were in shock. They urged me to hold off on any wedding plans until I was really sure of what I was doing. They asked us both to meet with their best friend who happened to be in London with her doctor husband. To please my parents, I agreed to the interview, although I felt that they were interfering unduly in the life of their 25-year-old son. I knew that my mother had secretly hoped I would marry the daughter of their friend, whom I had met in New York a few times three years earlier when I had visited my father in the hospital. I could sense that those meetings had been prearranged. The daughter seemed cold and sophisticated to me and I was not interested.

I was so sure that Miriam was the right person for me that we passed the interview in London with flying colors and my parents finally expressed their agreement.

I still had the planned trip to the continent ahead of me and invited Miriam to come along. While she was debating, she was informed by the medical examiner at the U.S. Consulate that a fungus infection on some of her toes had to be removed before she could be admitted as an immigrant to the USA. We were very upset. The procedure to remove the fungus would take several weeks and we were concerned that this might interfere with our wedding plans.

I shortened the continental trip of lab visits to which I was committed, in Holland, France and Switzerland. On the way from one lab to the next, I met with some comrades from the Ecole de Physique et de Chimie in Paris, bringing back happy memories of being accepted by them. In central France, I visited Eldy, the English lady who had tried in vain to make a cultured person out of me when I waited in Banyuls-sur-Mer for a U.S. immigration visa. In Switzerland, I saw my friend who had facilitated the correspondence with Edith in Paris during the war years.

I returned to London two days before the wedding, planned for August 21. We spent a honeymoon week at a lakeside hotel in the rugged and beautiful Scottish mountains, where the first flowers in the meadows appeared just as we arrived. It was still a time of food rationing in England, and carrots were the only vegetable available in the hotel. Every day, they were served for lunch and for dinner and ever since, I have not been able to eat carrots.

We went on many walks, hand in hand. We had each gone our separate way and had had our separate experiences. Since our teenage years, we both had been refugees away from our homes.

Over the years that have followed, we have had our individual joys and tragedies, our sharing of happy and sad experiences, and our quarrels, but we always kept our determination to stay together, not to be wanderers anymore, seeking refuge. The interlude in our lives had ended on August 21, 1947.

Before returning with Miriam to the U.S. on another converted troopship, I wrote a letter to one person in Urbana, that I was coming back as a married man, but whatever our relationship had been or would be, my affection and respect for her would remain intact. We avoided meeting again. Another interlude had come to an end.

11. Sam

SINCE I RETIRED eight years ago, I have tried to go for a walk every afternoon when the weather is nice, with Miriam if possible. If Sam is in his garden, he waves to me as I approach his house. He hopes I will play ball with him. He likes it best if I throw the ball high in the air and he catches it. Then he brings it back to me by rolling it down the driveway. If he is in a good mood, he will even bounce the ball so it doesn't get stuck in a rut that runs clear across the driveway.

Sam is eight years old. I like to talk to him, because he is a good listener. He doesn't say much, but by the way he looks at me I know we understand each other. When I first played with him several years ago, he used to get angry when I left to go home, but now he knows I play for about five minutes before I say, "one more time" and then, "this is the last time."

We have been through quite a bit together. Three years ago, I fell and broke my hip, not watching where I was going, intently thinking about Varian Fry, the American who helped my parents and me get out of France in 1940–41. I didn't lift my right foot high

85

enough when I stepped from the street onto the curb and fell, but I couldn't get up again. Luckily someone drove by and brought me home.

When I was in the hospital, Miriam sometimes walked by Sam's garden. He waved to her and looked down the street to see whether I might be coming. She told him it would be a while before I would return. He waited patiently, but the first day I limped by with a walker he brought me a ball. I told him, I couldn't bend down, but I could caress him a bit if he would let me, and he agreed.

Then, one day he was limping like me. He had a bandage around his leg. There were no balls in his garden, because he was not allowed to play. I just talked to him and told him we just have to cope with life despite our disabilities.

I knew that his mother had been a Labrador and his father a Golden Retriever. I wondered whether his mother had similar difficulties adapting to the different status of his father as mine had. And whether his father had died, as mine had. He had had a final heart attack in October 1951.

When my mother called me from Philadelphia, I was not completely unprepared because of my father's earlier attacks, but still it was a shock. In the spring, my parents had still visited us in Stanford Village where we were living at the time in one partition of a converted army hospital cottage. They wanted to see their two-year-old grandson and knew another grandchild was on the way. I could show them the house we were going to buy in Menlo Park. We did not want the children to grow up on the Stanford campus in an academic cocoon.

Of course, I immediately flew to Philadelphia and took care of the numerous arrangements which had to be made before and after my father's burial. Only when I returned home, was I conscious of feeling alone in the world. From here on, I would have to rely on myself, there was no one I could turn to in an emergency. I had to take complete responsibility, not only for my family, but also for my mother. I had not realized how much I had loved my father, but now it was too late to let him know about my feelings. I had not been able to express them to him earlier.

Sam listened to all this in silence. He did not know what to say. He probably thought that was a long time ago, long before he was born, and by now I should have gotten over my father's death and become the man my father had hoped.

The next time I saw Sam, he was tired out from a long walk he had with his owner. He wanted to play only for a little while, so I could just tell him that my mother died three years after my father in an automobile accident. She had moved to a suburb of Philadelphia to pursue her interests in drawing and painting, which had already developed when we were living in Berlin in the late twenties. They were interrupted by her duties as an institute director's wife in Heidelberg and subsequently by the flight to France and from there to the States. My father's death allowed her to again concentrate on her artistic talents. She coped with missing my father by learning how to teach and then teaching art to young children in a private school. She had hoped to move into our neighborhood at the end of the year, but that wish remained unfulfilled. I left Sam thinking I needed to tell him more.

A couple of years ago when I played with Sam, a man walked by. Sam growled and barked as I had never seen him do before. I said, "Sam, stop it, that man is just walking by and one doesn't just bark at people." The man turned out to be Sam's next-door neighbor. I guessed he didn't like Sam and had teased him, perhaps because Sam barked a lot when he was first left alone in his backyard. More recently, though, Sam has not barked when the same man walked by. Obviously, he was becoming more mature.

I was thinking about my own maturing. When I first started

teaching large freshman classes at Stanford in the late fifties, I used to close the doors to the auditorium as soon as the bell rang. I did not let in any students until I had finished a five-minute summary review of the previous lecture. During the lecture, if any students started talking or reading a newspaper, I asked them to leave. I felt, after spending many hours preparing each lecture and the pertinent demonstrations, the students owed it to me to give their full attention to the lecture for 45 minutes, and I told them so.

In the late sixties, the students became restless about the Vietnam War and Stanford went through a period of major demonstrations and even strikes, as many other universities did. The students believed that Stanford was supporting the war which they wanted to stop, through its scientific and engineering research programs. I organized a monthly series of evening talks by Physics and other science faculty, which I called "Physics and Man," to point out the beneficial effects to human beings from scientific research, misapplications not withstanding. I gave the first talk on "Physics and I." Over 200 students attended. (The talk is appended to this story.)

Even though one is always pressed for time in a freshman lecture course, I devoted a whole lecture to the experiences I had in Europe with dictatorship and expressed my opinion that human affairs should be governed by reason and not by dictates of any kind.

When the students later refused to enter classrooms in order to disrupt the university's teaching programs as much as possible, I sat outside the lecture hall, sometimes wrapped in a blanket against the early cold, and gave my lecture there. Luckily, after a while the students agreed that it was more comfortable to sit in lecture hall seats than on the ground or in rickety chairs. I did not close the doors any longer and let students in late, but not without glaring at them. Slowly I learned not to do that anymore.

Sometimes when I played with Sam, a young black cat watched us. She lived in the same house as Sam. When he was younger, he tried to chase her away when she rubbed against my legs and wanted to be gently stroked, and purred. In later years, he ignored her. He must have learned that it is important to get along with other beings.

I thought of all the people I have had to deal with in my professional life. As part of my desire to help disadvantaged persons, I was eager to further the educational development of minorities and women.

Early in my career at Stanford, I was able to offer an Assistant Professor position to a woman physicist, the first in our Department. I had hoped she would collaborate on some experiments, but she wanted to work completely independently. Thinking back how I reacted to my supervisor when I started a career at the University of Illinois, I could sympathize with her and left her alone. But, once I inquired, "How are things going?" She became very angry and accused me of checking up on her progress and wanting to dominate her work. I was completely baffled and decided I should not talk with her anymore, just nod when I pass her. She left at the end of the year. Fortunately, over the forty-odd years I was active at Stanford, I had more than a dozen young collaborators from whom I received much stimulation in a setting of pleasant relationships.

Once when I passed Sam's house, he was taking a nap in front of the door. As I passed by, he just opened one eye and then shut it again. He must have had some dreams which were more pleasant than the prospect of playing ball.

I also sometimes daydream about the pleasant times I have had in my life. When the boys were still babies, we were all invited by Miriam's mother to spend a couple of weeks in the summer at a beach house belonging to the Miramar Hotel in Santa Barbara. We were spoiled by having room service every day and could swim and laze as we wanted to. For the last fifty years, Miriam and I have revisited the same hotel occasionally and lately nearly every year.

As the boys grew older, we took them to many National Parks which bless the western part of the U.S. When they were six and eight years old, we went to Heidelberg, where I had spent my youth. Miriam and I still laugh when we recall how in a streetcar a middle-aged lady said to our younger son in German, "Won't you get up from your seat for a lady?" and he answered, *"Ich spreche nicht Deutsch."* ("I don't speak German.")

When I was sixty years old and the boys had established their lives, I asked myself what would still be fun to do while my health permits. I decided to learn sailing. I bought some books about the techniques of handling small sailboats, how to read the wind direction from small flags on the mast and the mainsail and from the direction of the waves, how to turn the boat and sail against the wind and then with the wind. I started practicing on a small lake in the Santa Cruz mountains and gradually explored more challenging waters near Foster City. I rented boats which were faster and which needed to be handled more precisely. One type of boat was called LASER. To keep it from tipping over one had to lean far over the side of the boat while pulling on the rope which controls the pitch of the mainsail. It was exhilarating to skim over the water and sail under bridges which just cleared the top of the mast.

Although Miriam did not want to come along, she let me take her out on a broad-bottomed boat when we were on vacation in San Diego. We were reminded of our punting trip in Oxford forty years earlier.

My sailing career ended ignominiously ten years later, when one Sunday afternoon a Swiss visitor and I each took a LASER to the edge of the San Francisco Bay. The weather was beautiful and the wind conditions just right, so we ventured further into the Bay.

When we decided to turn back, the wind had increased enough that I could no longer handle my boat and it tipped over. I had learned how to right it and climbed back in.

Then I wanted to help my friend whose boat had lost its rudder in the rough water, but before I could reach him, my boat tipped over once more. After this happened for the fourth time, I was so exhausted with my seventy years of age, that I could no longer right the boat and climb in. Fortunately, a large sailboat had observed my dilemma and picked me up, towing my upside down sailboat behind. I was wrapped in a blanket despite my protest that I was okay. Meanwhile the boat had radioed the Coast Guard which sent a helicopter, lowering a basket and ordering me to climb in. I was brought to the Stanford Hospital where a nurse determined that my temperature was just one degree above the point where I needed to be treated for hypothermia.

Miriam picked me up in the evening and we drove to the boat dock where my friend had just arrived, having been able by body motion to steer his rudderless boat into the coastal silt. Years before, he had taken a thorough Swiss training course in sailing techniques.

When I passed Sam's garden again I thought, "Last time you missed a good story." But he still was not interested in playing with me. He just wanted to continue dreaming his happy dreams.

When I passed my sixty-fifth birthday, I also had a happy dream. I thought it would be enjoyable to do one physics experiment at the two-mile Stanford Linear Accelerator before I ended my career at Stanford. I read in the literature to see what type of experiment would fit my experience and after a year of searching found an article involving an effect producing x-rays with which I had worked for many years. I thought with modern equipment one could do a better experiment on the effect, and started making calculations.

Then one day, while calculating, I had an idea which would measure the effect one hundred times better than had been done before. I prepared a proposal to the director of the Stanford accelerator. After a thorough scientific review, we were granted up to 48 hours of beam time, just to test the idea. As soon as it was determined that the idea worked, we were supposed to stop and let the next experimental group have the beam, because beam time is so precious and expensive. We would then be given another 48-hour time period for the main experiment at a later time, but if the idea did not work, that would be the end for us.

As part of the complicated experimental setup, we had to string electrical cables from the floor to a counting room five stories up, where we would be protected from nuclear radiation during the accelerator operation. I remember hanging on a metal ladder going straight up the wall like a fire escape, secured by a rope around my body and the ladder. Moving up the ladder, rung by rung, at the end, I was dangling fifty feet above floor, holding on to the ladder with one hand and with the other hand pulling the cables up.

After a two-month set-up period, when the accelerator was turned on for us one morning, the x-ray signals were so clear, that by the evening I knew my idea would work. I was battling with my conscience whether to continue or to turn over the accelerator to the next experimental group, but finally I told myself that nobody would want to start another experiment in the night.

Instead, I said to my young collaborators, most of them enthusiastic undergraduates (graduate students had shied away from me because of my age), "Let's go ahead and try to do the main experiment. Are you willing to spend the next two nights without sleep?" and they all agreed. Every hour, two of them had to run down five floors of steps, make a small change on the apparatus and run up five floors of steps, before the beam could be turned on again and our measurements could be continued.

At the end of the 48-hour period, I was exhausted and exhilarated. It was the first experiment I had done in fifty years which worked right away and sooner than I had anticipated. The next day, I wrote to the director of the accelerator and told him about our results, and he forgave me for violating the strict conditions for the beam time. We were also given another 48 hours of beam time a year later, when we were better prepared.

Lately when I have passed Sam's garden, he has been sleeping with his face turned away from the street. Like me, he has been seeking a simpler life. No longer am I dashing from one scientific meeting to the next, anxious to present new and interesting research results. In between, I had worried how to divide my time between the pleasures and demands of the family and those of my professional life. When I was younger, the latter won out. As soon as I came home in late afternoon, I went into my study to work. During dinner, I was so preoccupied that I could hardly listen to the conversation. Then I would return to my study to continue the calculations or prepare my next lecture, until midnight or later.

Only since my retirement have I made attempts to change my habits. For more than fifty years, Miriam has patiently endured my one-track mind, always supporting my work. How could I have been more fortunate, Sam?

The last time I saw Sam, I found him exhausted after catching just three balls. I tried to console him that being old also has many benefits. You can follow your own interests and don't have to do something because you want to measure up to your or others' expectations. If, at some time you want to write about your life, you can do that, or if you want to take a nap, that's okay too. And, you don't have to tell everything. "There are some things you don't want to tell, aren't there?" I asked Sam. He looked at me, but did not answer.

Phisics and I, Stanford University, May 5, 1970

To understand how I ended up as a physicist, I have to tell you something about my background. My father came from a family of upper-class clothing merchants, who valued intellectual activity. He was a biochemist, or more particularly, a physiologist. He was interested mainly in the physical and chemical processes which occur during muscle contraction and expansion. I recall how he took me to his lab to show me an apparatus which measured the contraction of frog muscles stimulated electrically. My thoughts at the time were more in sympathy with the frogs than with the muscles. Perhaps because of this, my first inclination at age five, was to become a streetcar conductor. By age eight, I found carpentry more interesting. All my life, I have enjoyed woodwork.

By the time I was 12, I started to collect minerals. Then I got interested in chemistry. My brother and I had a small lab in our house. We conducted all kinds of experiments, including electrolysis of water under a bell jar. Since we did not separate the hydrogen and the oxygen, that particular experiment had a spectacular ending. The bell jar blew into a thousand pieces, but for some reason neither one of us was injured.

You can understand, though, that I didn't feel comfortable about chemistry after that. Physics seemed safer. The final push was given to me by a high school teacher who let me come into the physics lab after school. I was in England at the time, and felt fairly lonely as a boarder. So I tinkered around with the physics lab equipment and performed some leisurely experiments.

My formal physics education started in Paris in 1939, and, with various interruptions, ended at the University of Pennsylvania with a Ph.D. I always liked experimentation and got involved in it to various degrees early in my graduate years. Nowadays, I see many students discouraged by the prospect of four years of college followed by another four or five years of graduate study. If these students would just show a little initiative and get themselves a job in a research lab—any job, and without pay at first—they would soon find themselves drawn into some kind of meaningful activity and get to feel some of the excitement which accompanies research and discovery. Studying is then much easier, even though one seems to have less time for it. And the advantage of a university over a college is that such opportunities exist.

This brings me to the question of why I like physics. Right off, I should say that I like physics only in an academic setting. I find students very stimulating and necessary to keep me from mental decay. This benefit is not available anywhere except at a university. During the Second World War I worked in an industrial laboratory and also for several years I was a consultant for an oil company. I can recognize the satisfaction that stems from doing something which is immediately practical. But, I prefer the university life in which I am driven by my own goals rather than someone else's.

I am now halfway through my academic life. I have been active in research and teaching for about twenty years and I have another twenty to go before I retire. Teaching has always given me a deep satisfaction, but if I look back over the past twenty years, my greatest thrills, and greatest depressions, have come in my research work. When after half a year or a year of failures, one finally licks a problem one has set oneself, a tremendous elation and personal gratification occurs, which is typical of all creative accomplishments. In scientific work, though, if one has done one's job well, there is an element of certainty about the fact one has wrung from nature, which is absent from other human activities. This is because the method of scientific inquiry assures one usually of a yes/no type of answer: either the experiment agrees with theory or it does not.

My own work as a graduate student was connected with the

properties of contacts between a metal and a semiconductor. To this day I regret that I wasn't a bit smarter and discovered the transistor. After my Ph.D. thesis, I switched to nuclear physics, because I wanted to study something new. My present research, like that of most nuclear physicists, deals with the role of nuclear forces in determining the motions of nuclear particles within the nucleus. I don't know whether the results I obtain will have any practical consequences, but I am not really concerned. In a minute, I'll discuss the reason for this attitude.

During the second half of my academic life, I can see teaching becoming of greater and greater importance to me. I feel that in the present situation in which there is so much uncertainty and struggle in the world, I should devote more time to students than before. Young people are particularly sensitive to the underlying problems of society, but they are frustrated that solutions are not immediately available. Perhaps the experience of an adult person can provide some measure of stability. Also, many young people have become disenchanted with science. Perhaps I can rekindle some enthusiasm for physics. But, to be a good teacher, I must be able to bring new discoveries into the classroom. Since physics is a science which continually changes and progresses, I must keep up with new developments. This can best be done if I am involved in research, and so I will continue to do this, but perhaps with a lesser intensity than when I was younger. A couple of years ago, I wrote a textbook on nuclear physics. This involves a lot of drudgery, but when it finally appeared in print, I felt proud and pleased. If it is successful, I'll be even more pleased and might be enticed to write more.

Let me now discuss how as a human being I justify my role as a physicist. Like most scientists, the attitude I have about my work is neither wholly selfish nor wholly self-effacing. I obtain satisfaction from fruitful research, but I also hope for approval from my peers. Similarly, I am pleased if my teaching is good, but I am more gratified if my students appreciate what I am doing. Beyond these personal feelings, I have the deep conviction that my role in the community of scientists will benefit humanity. Even though my particular work may make only an infinitesimal or zero contribution, I believe that collectively science helps man overcome ignorance and want. Public affairs, esthetic standards, religious beliefs, in other words, all elements of culture have been influenced by science. The cause of this deep impact is the revolution science has wrought in our fundamental views of reality. Astronomers and physicists have discovered a universe of galaxies and atoms that challenge earlier notions of the world around us. Thanks to science, man's thinking has become less orthodox, more skeptical and more receptive to new ideas. Thanks to science, technology has been able to develop and, on the whole, technology has eased man's burden, even though it may produce some burdens of its own. I have no doubt that science has made man more secure about himself in relation to nature, even though it is virtually certain that in other parts of the universe life also exists and that man is not unique.

Let's see now how science has influenced the other activities of the human spirit, such as art and religion. Science and art both draw on creative inspiration, but science helps man to know, whereas art teaches him to feel. Science has encouraged the artist to wider experimentation and has given him a better understanding of his tools. Science confirms the premise of religion that the universe and man are created for an orderly purpose. But religion alone can give us the principles of human morals and suggest what our purpose might be. Science has destroyed much of the dogma of religion, but, at the same time, the seemingly unending complexities of nature instill man with a new feeing of humility which is in accord with religious teaching.

In thinking about the unending complexity of nature, I am wondering whether one of the causes of student revolt these days isn't against the unending accumulation of knowledge. How difficult it is to cope with all this knowledge—isn't it simpler to ignore it all and take LSD. As a scientist I would say, though, consider how little is known and how exciting it is to bring a little knowledge to the surface!

Finally, you may want to know what person I am. I am not really much different from other human beings and have my periods of gaiety and grief, certainty and bafflement, triumph and defeat. In the 1950s, researches were made about U.S. scientists. Although I was not interviewed, many of the characteristics found are also applicable to me. (This material is taken from a Life Science Library book entitled *The Scientist*.)

First of all, the scientist has a general need for independence, autonomy and for personal mastery of the environment. (No wonder university presidents age early.) He doesn't like conformity in thinking. He loves seemingly contradictory facts or ideas and is challenged by resolving them.

Emotionally, he is at the same time stable and sensitive. Although he may be critical of others, he avoids personal controversies. The research scientist has a strong ego. This sometimes makes him overly dignified and may cause him to keep an unduly tight rein on himself. He is usually not impulsive and talkative.

In his younger years, he usually develops a precocious self-confidence about solving intellectual problems. His family almost invariably sets a great score on book learning. As an adult, he is open minded about religion. Although not agnostic, he is skeptical about orthodox doctrines. For this reason perhaps, there are fewer Catholic scientists than Protestant and Jewish.

As a member of the community, a scientist pays at least as much attention to civic duties as the average man does. This is certainly true in our Physics Department. My own civic activities have a sinusoidal time dependence with a period of a few years. I have been active in political campaigns and civil rights organizations. Although at the moment I am in a trough of civic activity, I can feel a positive slope approaching as the election nears.

Meanwhile, I feel free to pursue my hobbies, the most intense of which is skiing. In fact, in a few hours I should be heading to the Sierras and give vent to my nonscientific pleasure.

12. The Crate

FOR MORE THAN FORTY YEARS the crate stood on its side in our garage, gathering dust and serving only as a support for some tools I wanted to keep handy. When it arrived, I had pried open part of the lid and took out some correspondence my mother had saved and which looked interesting to me at the time, because it dealt with the period from 1938 to 1941 when my parents and I fled from Germany to France and from there to the U.S. The bulk of the contents consisted of a dozen large art folders and a couple of coffee table books, which I never looked at in detail because I had been too busy. Most of the folders seemed to be filled with my mother's sketches and watercolors, too much to look at.

Now I am seventy-eight years old and am writing stories about my life. My mother's personality is woven through these stories and is still occupying me. I seem to have a need to understand her better before my life feels complete. Maybe it never will, but I want to find out whether her artistic interests and endeavors reveal any clues to broaden my understanding.

The crate is not yielding its secrets easily. It is so heavy for me now, that I can hardly tip it over onto the garage floor. Once on the floor, I bend over only with difficulty. I put on some gardener's gloves and brush off the layers of dust which have settled on everything, in the same way as I hope to brush off a few layers of memory of my mother's life. Besides the art folders, I find a dozen smaller sketch books with charcoal and crayon sketches and watercolor paintings. One file contains a few oil paintings. Nothing is dated or signed.

A large envelope contains letters from my mother to my father, most from the period August 1944 to the end of 1945, and one from 1946. I struggle for days with the question whether I would violate my mother's privacy if I read these letters which came into my possession by chance, because she died in an automobile accident in 1954. The crate had been sent to me by the executors of her estate.

My father had had a heart attack in the summer of 1944 while he and my mother were in Woods Hole, MA. My father, besides vacationing, also had been given office space at the Marine Biological Laboratory there. My mother, my sister, a sister of my father and the wife of a doctor friend who also spent the summer in Woods Hole, all took turns sharing the demanding care for my father after his hospital stay. My mother was able to return periodically to our apartment in Philadelphia and wrote to my father from there. He must have kept the letters, because he and my mother had hardly ever been separated and he must have treasured the letters. She must have found them when he died in 1951, and, in turn, kept them as a remembrance.

$\mathfrak{c}$

In the last Life Stories class, I asked my classmates whether they had ever been in a situation similar to mine, and what would they or did they do if faced with the question whether it is right to invade our parents' privacy if we accidentally find their correspondence. One person said she had faced a similar dilemma and opt-ed to read one letter, on the basis of which she decided not to read any more. Another person took the view that she was interested in what the letters would reveal about her life, and read all the corre-spondence. But then she found the letters raised questions which she would have liked to discuss with her parents but no longer could.

I contemplated these thoughtful responses and decided I would read one dated letter by my mother (many were not dated) and then decide how to proceed. I am glad I did, because I found that my mother really did not express many intimacies with my father, but mainly reported on her daily activities in Philadelphia, on the times she would arrive in Woods Hole again and how much she was looking forward to her visit and what she could bring.

In one letter, she complained that there was a loud radio blar-ing in front of her bedroom window. At first she did not see any person connected with the radio, but then discovered a young man and very much wished that instead of changing the stations all the time, he would change the volume. Evidently, she was too timid to go outside and tell him to lower the sound level. For me, it was important that the letters clarified my mother's art activities in Philadelphia, which I had not remembered.

ჯ

During the unpacking of the crate, a piece of paper fluttered out of one of the folders on which my mother had copied some sen-tences describing her own feelings about art. The paper evidently was precious to her because she had carefully mended a tear with a bit of scotch tape.

Painting isn't just something you see with your eyes. It's something you feel with your *whole body*. It is the design of

your hurt or your happiness and when other people see it
they feel the hurt or the happiness as you did.

She does not quote the source, but I am wondering whether I can
still feel art with my whole body, or whether a deeper understanding of my mother's hurt and happiness will escape me. In my adolescent years, I actually made quite good ink sketches thanks to the
tutoring by one of my internment camp companions in France,
who was an accomplished painter. But, in my later years, I let my
artistic talents slide.

℘

My earliest remembrance of my mother's interest in art dates from
Berlin, where we lived in the 1920s until I was seven years old. My
mother took drawing lessons from Johannes Itten, in Germany a
prominent art teacher, originally connected with the Bauhaus
movement. At the time, Itten believed that before going on to col-
or, one should learn about form, shape and shadow by using charcoal. My mother sometimes took me along, and I made charcoal
drawings by her side.

In the crate there was a large, heavy book by Itten entitled
Tagebuch (Diary), of which he dedicated a numbered copy to my
mother in 1949 when my mother already was in the U.S. The book
was handwritten by him in 1930 in large Gothic German script
and is profusely illustrated with his and others, charcoal or black
and white drawings. Only 300 copies were privately printed and
bound at the Itten School. The dedication to my mother was
something special and shows that Itten had remembered my
mother after more than twenty years.

Although none of my mother's drawings from that time remain, I can recognize the Itten style in her later drawings. There
are charcoal nudes with beautiful shapes and soft shadows graded
with a soft-leather tipped tool used in charcoal work. Also, with a

single stroke of the crayon in a black and white sketch, she could indicate the shape and shadows of a sailboat gliding on the water.

I do not recall any artistic activity on her part when we later lived in Heidelberg and she had to fulfill the duties of an Institute Director's wife, nor in Paris where we did not have any help. Household duties and then the flight to southern France and from there to the U.S. took all her energies. In Heidelberg and in Paris she made intimate friendships with some artists. She devoted practically all her energies to my father's life. He reciprocated her devotion with deep respect and love, often expressed in poems.

After settling down in Philadelphia, where my parents arrived in October 1940, and after getting me there from France in mid-1941, my mother could return to her artistic interests. By 1944, as I learned from her letters to my father, she was taking art lessons which taught her about the use of color. Also, she was a very active volunteer in an art museum, teaching children about the imaginative use of art. She was very pleased and felt very much appreciated when on her office door in the art museum one day she found a label "Hedwig Meyerhof, Assistant Art Instructor." She reported proudly that within a few years the number of children attending the classes she was helping to teach had increased from just a few to over fifty.

After my father's death in October 1951, she did not want to remain in our apartment in Philadelphia and moved to Haverford, a suburb where she found a job in a Quaker school, teaching art to preteen children. In the summer of 1952, she attended a course given by Hans Hofman, a famous art teacher in Provincetown, MA. From him she learned more about the use of vivid colors in expressing feeling and imagination, and how to teach art.

Since all my mother's sketches, drawings and watercolors are undated, I cannot tell which ones were done at Hofman's school and which ones were made earlier or later. There are some very geometrical pencil drawings, mostly in graded black and white, some sketches of bone structure and some color scales, which must have been exercises suggested by Hofman. In all, there are about fifty pictures from very rough and, to me, confused color arrangements, to beautiful scenes of lakes and coastal regions. Many of these have trees penciled in, in a manner very similar to what I found in Itten's *Diary*.

The change of care taken in making a particular picture must reflect a change in mood, depending on whether my mother felt her own hurt or her happiness. Throughout my life, especially when I was young, these swings in her mood have caused similar swings in my emotions.

In one folder, I found a short poem about nature. Every second line or so has a child's name written next to it. I imagine in her class at the Quaker school, she read the poem out loud, and let each child choose the part of the poem he wished to illustrate. The children loved this gentle guidance of their imagination. This way of teaching art must also have been appreciated by other art teachers, because her children's paintings were among those chosen for a special exhibit of children's art at the New York Museum of Modern Art.

I remember a warm and appreciative letter from the head of the Quaker school saying how much the children missed my mother when she was killed in 1954, driving back to her apartment after working on art therapy with children in a nearby hospital.

ℊ

So, what have I learned about my mother by reviewing her art? I think her work confirms what I had known, that despite deep and lasting struggles in her life, at other times she was absolutely sure of her role, as sure as the stroke of a brush or crayon with which she could indicate a whole scene. Also, the mere fact that she could single-mindedly pursue her interest in art as her own special activity indicates an ability to persist in fulfilling a personal desire.

The same ability already expressed itself in the years before her marriage, when as the only one, and youngest, of five children of a middle-class merchant family she pursued the study of mathematics and physics at a time when women generally did not go to the university, let alone study scientific subjects.

Although I have urges to want to know more, I feel at this point I should leave my mother some privacy and not delve more into her personality and life. I have decided to select those of her pictures which I find the most interesting and expressive and put them in a more dignified place than a dusty, open crate in the garage, so that other descendents may appreciate and enjoy them.

g

Now, I right up the empty crate with physical ease and put it back into its former place in the garage, feeling also a mental ease that I have been able to add a small measure of love and devotion to a person who spent a large part of her life bringing so much more of those to her family and to others.